CW01656596

SEA

Other titles available in this series

THE SMALL ROCK GARDEN – E. B. Anderson
DO-IT-YOURSELF IN THE GARDEN – Barry Bucknell
FRUIT FOR SMALL GARDENS – Howard H. Crane
WINDOW-BOX GARDENING – Xenia Field
THE SMALL GREENHOUSE – H. G. Witham Fogg
THE KITCHEN GARDEN – Brian Furner
BULBS FOR SMALL GARDENS – E. C. M. Haes
FLOWERS FROM SEED – Denis Hardwicke
PERENNIAL FLOWERS FOR SMALL GARDENS – Peter Hunt
GARDENING IN THE NORTH – Kenneth Lemmon
THE SMALL GARDEN – C. E. Lucas Phillips
DAHLIAS FOR SMALL GARDENS – James E. Rooke
CHRYSANTHEMUMS FOR SMALL GARDENS – James F. Smith
GARDENING FOR THE ELDERLY AND HANDICAPPED – Leslie Snook
GARDENING ON CHALK AND LIME – Christopher Lloyd
RHODODENDRONS FOR SMALL GARDENS – Eric Joy

Pan Piper Small Garden Series

Editor: C. E. Lucas Phillips

GARDENING BY THE SEA

J. R. B. Evison

A PAN ORIGINAL

PAN BOOKS LTD : LONDON

First Published 1969 by Pan Books Ltd.,
33 Tothill Street, London, S.W.1.

330 02244 X

Printed in Great Britain by
Cox & Wyman Ltd
London, Reading and Fakenham

CONTENTS

ILLUSTRATIONS IN PHOTOGRAVURE

Chapter 1

IN PERIL BY THE SEA

THE UNHOLY TRINITY – COASTAL SOILS – SEASIDE CLIMATES

This is the story of a battle. A story as old as man himself, for it is that which he wages with the elements around him.

Imagine, if you will, a wild night with the wind rising and high seas running. Man and beast will take shelter from the fury that is to come as the tide rises. Our plants cannot do likewise, however, but must fend for themselves and tomorrow we shall look for damage. Over everything in the path of the storm – buildings, glasshouses, cars, ironwork or plants – will be a film of salty moisture, sticky to the touch and difficult to clean from windows or cars. How far back these conditions will extend depends on the fury of the gale. The worst coastal storm in my experience, in July 1956, showed damage up to twelve miles from the shore. This is most exceptional; real trouble is usually confined to a few hundred yards from the shore.

I have painted this gloomy picture as I find that those who have not experienced such storms are apt to picture gardens beside the sea in terms of sunny summer days which formed part of a contented holiday. Even as holidays are fleeting so are perfect days; winds, too, are by no means the prerogative of winter. But it is far from my purpose to so labour the storm as to give the impression that a garden by the sea is a hopeless project. Rather would I have you realize that you must put your hand in the hand of Nature and accept her guidance.

Let us then look at the antidote to these problems. It is *shelter*. In the pages which follow I hope to show that, given this boon, gardening by the sea is easy and most rewarding.

The Unholy Trinity

Coastal gardens have one advantage over all other gardens in that the sea is much more reluctant to give up its warmth at night than is the land. The practical result of this is that for a few miles from the coast temperatures are several degrees higher than inland, making it possible to grow species more sensitive to temperature.

Unfortunately, coastal gardens are subject to a less attractive phenomenon of nature – ***the wind***. Few without actual experience of its power can appreciate its ability to lash the sea into mountainous waves, to pick up and bear along spray as a cruel weapon with which to batter all things living in its path, actually to rub salt in the wounds so caused. A wind which can blow in plate-glass windows, blow down the best rooted of trees, or snap off a car door incautiously opened. Flowers may be broken, fruit trees seriously damaged, and bees and other pollinating insects may be unable to fly at critical times. It is small wonder that there are few plants that survive such treatment unprotected, and those which do are often twisted and contorted caricatures of their true selves.

Of course, coastal dwellers have no monopoly of high winds – any dweller in exposed places faces much the same problem where wind velocity is concerned and the same remedies which will be outlined later are open to them.

Staking of herbaceous plants, dahlias, etc, needs to be attended to earlier, to be more substantial and have the tying-in of new growth done more frequently. The devastating dessication which persistent and drying winds can cause is but little recognized and may well be the villain in many a mysterious death. Even greenhouse plants may suffer through the wind, for it can cause such a drop in temperature that, in the lack of a really efficient heating system, the plants within may be harmed.

Certain factors make storms at the seaside especially damaging, for high winds will carry with them any object light enough to be borne along. The most to be feared are ***sand*** and ***salt***.

Sand is much less common but where the normal tides do not cover all of a sandy beach at high tide, or where dunes are present, loose sand may be swept up by violent winds to blast and chisel and tear at all plants in its path. This is quite the most abrasive of all forms of damage. Fortunately, because it is rarely carried to a great height, shelter devices are more successful than in the case of spray.

The actual damage caused by wind-borne spray is the result of physical battering by this weapon and is not dissimilar to that caused by wind-borne rain. The ultimate harm is much greater, for the strong salt solution in an open wound induces plasmolysis or reverse osmosis of tissues deeper than those injured and may result in the death of vital plant parts.

Some curious side effects can arise out of maltreatment of plants by bad weather. I have referred already to an unusual storm in July 1956, possibly the most violent of the century. In the course of it many trees were totally defoliated on the windward side – a phenomenon which clearly deceived many a tree. I shall never forget seeing a horse chestnut the following October with its crop of 'conkers' on one side and a multitude of flowers on the other – the windward – side. Many a fruit tree flowered that autumn concurrently with its fruit and it was not unusual to see laburnum, cherry and pyrus in flower in October.

These then are your enemies. Know them and you may defeat them more easily.

Coastal Soils

Coastal soils are infinitely variable, from the silty clays of parts of Essex to the light sands of districts of Hampshire, where they have formed a good home for the pines which are such a characteristic feature of Bournemouth. Large areas, too, on the east coast and on the south coast from Brighton to Dover are alkaline; chalk has been formed by the skeletons of myriads of sea creatures who lived and died in the warm waters which once covered the area of the North and South Downs. No places these for lovers of the rhododendron and camellia. For them the south-west and western coasts, which are mainly acid and there are relatively few areas where these plants do not flourish.

Few buy a house for the garden, however, and the real art of the gardener is to adapt his soil to the plants he wishes to grow or to choose those plants which enjoy the existing soil. Gardeners of sandy soils should note that there are scarcely any plants which refuse to grow in them; they are warm, and therefore early; plants root readily and grow quickly given adequate food. The latter is best supplied by digging in plenty of humus to increase the water retention and by using slow-dissolving fertilizers – usually of natural or organic origin, like bone meal. Humus helps with watering problems also, as it retains that which comes naturally in the form of rain and reduces the need for frequent artificial watering, which is all too often necessary on light soils.

The above remarks apply also to chalky soils. Where plants have especial preferences reference is made in the descriptive lists in this book. In the absence of such a guide the plant will grow on any soil type.

Seaside Climates

If by climate we mean the admixture of temperature and

rainfall often masquerading as 'weather', it is most certainly critical to the gardener and, for a small island, we certainly have our fair share of variability. Being roughly triangular, we have eastern, southern, and western coasts to consider.

If one were to take at face value the often-repeated statement that the eastern coast is bleak, cold, windswept, and dry, one would be party to a complete fallacy. True, it does have its share of wind, but success is there for those who create shelter or make use of what is there. It may be drier, but who will complain if it is not eternally raining? A by-product is that frost seems less damaging; hard growth and little moisture to turn into ice see to this. You will be hard put to find better-coloured roses than in coastal Essex; Scarborough has *Olearia traversii* and *O. macrodonta* growing happily and how many cliff-tops can boast red-hot-pokers as good as those at Whitley Bay? With a little more attention to shelter, some adventure in planting might yield surprising results.

The southern coast is dry and has the best light of any of our coasts, but is not outstandingly warm. Kent is one of our snowiest counties, while 20° of frost are not exceptional in other parts. A good coast on which to grow choice plants, it changes character as soon as the hills of Devon appear. From Sidmouth westwards all is conditioned by the warm western rain-bearing winds and the warm water of the Gulf Stream. So we have conditions which are predominantly wet and warm together with a heavily indented coast giving sheltered valleys on mainly acid soils, in which lush and lusty growth abounds. Anyone who has been to the Gibson's garden at Rhu and seen century-old rhododendrons 50 to 60 ft high and as much through or *Magnolia campbellii* in Cornwall high as a house, can appreciate that this coast has the conditions nearest to a gardening paradise that men are likely to find.

Chapter 2

THE ANTIDOTES

SNARES OF SOLID WALLS – WIND-FILTERING FENCES – LIVING SHELTER FOR SUMMER – PLANTS PROTECTED BY NATURE – ZONES OF PROTECTION – STABILIZING SAND, SHINGLE AND CLIFFS

Quite simply, seaside gardening is easy if you can provide shelter. Let us look at the means by which this can be done.

Few of us can choose a site; usually we have to garden on sites developed by others. It is doubtful if anyone who has gardened right on the shore would recommend anyone else to try it. Rather they would encourage the newcomer to retire behind a barrier – a hill, a depression in the ground, a woodland, other buildings, or anything that will act as a primary filter to the first fury of the wind. Such a move will at least remove the danger from sand, which is dropped at the first impediment in a wind's path.

It is wise to remember that any 'wonderful view of the sea' is double-ended; the sea has an equally good sight of you, as you may find to your cost when a gale decides to throw itself at you from seaward. Unfortunately spray is not so easily held back as sand, for it may be borne for some miles inland, but in practical terms the real danger is within 400–500 yds of the water's edge.

The Snares of Solid Walls

So we come to the real problem of seaside gardening: the provision of protection from the winds that blow and anything they may carry with them.

Reduced to its simplest terms, this is best done not by a wall, as one might well imagine, but by a semi-permeable barrier which will filter the wind rather than arrest it.

The facts about walls and other solid barriers need explaining and are worth a little study, as an understanding of their effects reveals a number of ways in which their properties can be turned to good account by the gardener beside the sea.

The reaction of any human being in trying to obtain shelter from the gale would be to crawl into the protection of a solid wall, be it house, breakwater, wall, solid thick hedge, or similar barrier. Why, then, should this not be suitable for plants? In fact it is so if one is concerned only with the area occupied by a man standing in the wall's immediate shelter; but, garden walls are usually expected to protect a stretch of the garden many times their own height – a very different brief.

A wall may be expected to give good shelter to a distance of about twice its height, *ie*, a 5-ft wall may protect for 10 ft. In the next 10 ft comes the real reason to fear

walls, for the wind, thwarted and diverted upwards by the barrier, swoops down with awesome force in a series of swirls and eddies which form an area of intense turbulence. Damage so caused may easily be greater than the original storm would have created. A diagrammatic representation of this wind pattern is shown on page 17.

So no wall for the wise man, but what else?

All the evidence is that a semi-permeable barrier gives the best results. An example of such a fence might be a framework supporting slats of wood 1 in. wide with spaces 1 in. wide between each. Thus the barrier is half solid and half space and near to the theoretical optimum degree of permeability – 48 per cent.

Look at the diagram on page 19. You will observe that, instead of the area of intense turbulence caused by a solid wall or fence, you now have an area of reduced velocity. A barrier such as this can bring down wind speeds dramatically. A 50-mile-per-hour wind can be reduced to 10 miles-per-hour at a distance up to four times the height of the barriers. From here on, there will be a gradual increase in wind velocity until the original wind force is resumed at a distance about thirty to forty times the height of the fence. So at this place another similar barrier must be erected if more protection is needed.

Two other observations are worth making in the sketch illustrating wind patterns made by the solid wall. From the directions of the arrows you will see that what amounts to a cushion of air builds up in front of the wall causing the high wind to rise steeply. Thus there is a calm area immediately in *front* of the wall where plants often grow quite well.

Still more bizarre is the success with which low-growing plants can grow on *top* of such a wall. The air leaps up and over, leaving the plant to flourish in apparently the worst possible place.

Yet another place where the mechanics of the wind's progress make life tolerable for a few plants is the few inches nearest the ground when this is flat or nearly so. An

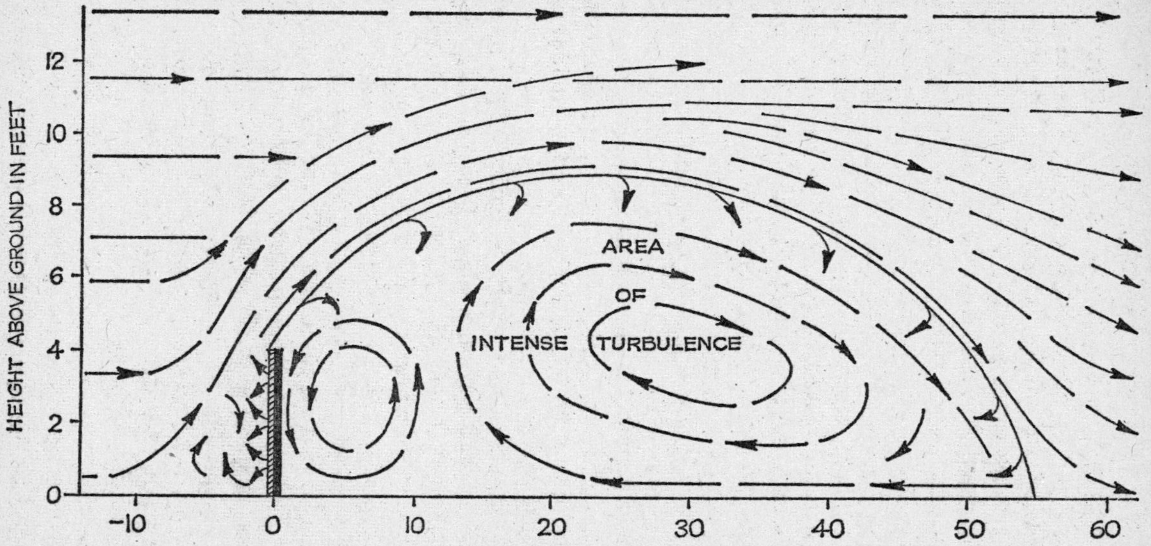

Wind pattern arising from a solid barrier

area of low pressure builds up in which naturally dwarf plants, or those made dwarf by the searing of their young growths by the winds, will flourish and flower in apparently full exposure. The success of gazanias and mesembryanthemums in such places illustrates this.

There are several ways in which you can make your own barriers, the choice depending on the finance available and the degree of informality you think necessary or desirable. They may be formed from living material, such as shrubs, trees, and hedges, or they may be artificial barriers and these we shall consider first. The others deserve separate chapters to themselves.

Wind-filtering Fences

A suitable permeable fence will do three desirable things:

1. As already explained, it will reduce the speed of the wind up to one-fifth of the original speed, up to four times the height of the barrier.

2. It will provide shelter for as much as forty times its own height, *ie*, a 4-ft fence might offer some shelter up to 160 ft, but not at the high level of efficiency mentioned in (1). Wind speed will gradually rise again, so that at 160 ft it will probably be back to 90 per cent of the original.

3. It will cause far less of that unfortunate by-product of the solid barrier, turbulence. The nearer the fence or barrier is to solidity the more turbulence occurs.

Experiments seem to show that barriers with about 40 per cent aperture to 60 per cent solid give the most satisfactory balance between shelter and lack of turbulence. See pages 20 and 21.

Gales do not blow every day and it may be more convenient to improve existing shelter by the use of temporary, moveable fences which can be put up when high winds threaten. For example, wattle hurdles are available in most

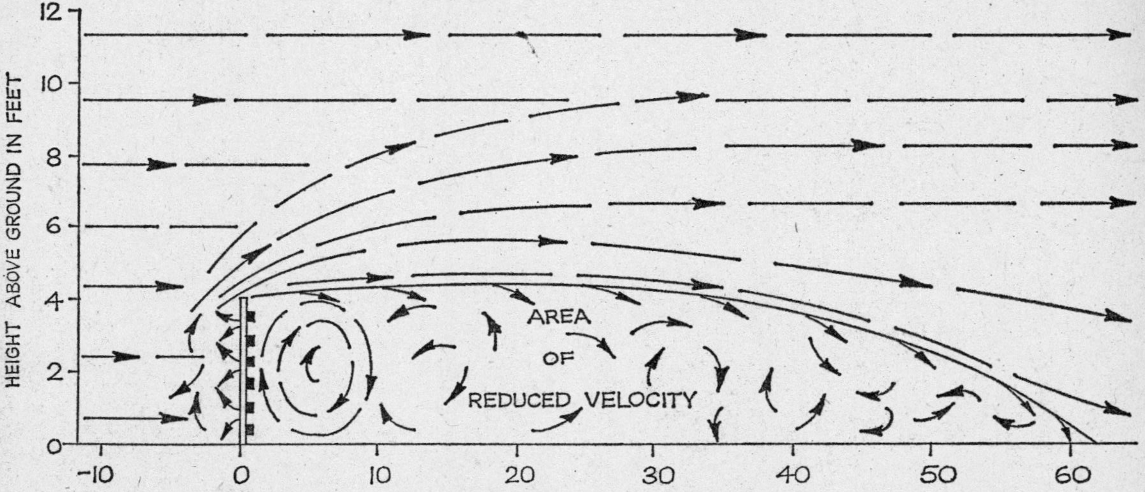

Wind pattern arising from a semi-permeable barrier

districts and, although they are more solid than is really desirable, they do make a reasonable barrier. Their best friends would not call them beautiful so, if they are erected

1. Framework fencing with branches of pine, gorse, etc, fixed to it.

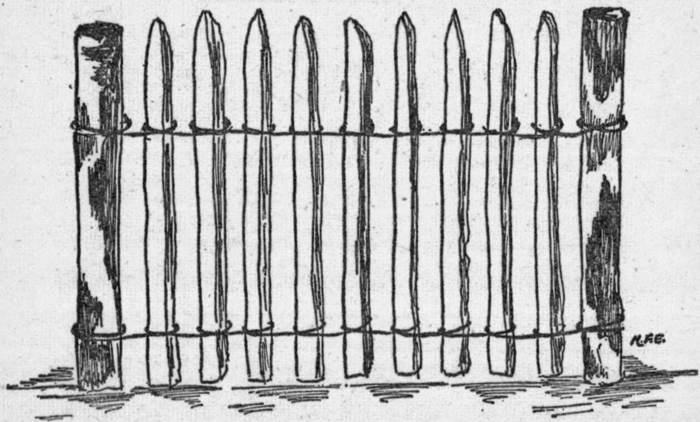

2. Chestnut paling ('chespale'), specially made with spaces equivalent to the width of the pales.

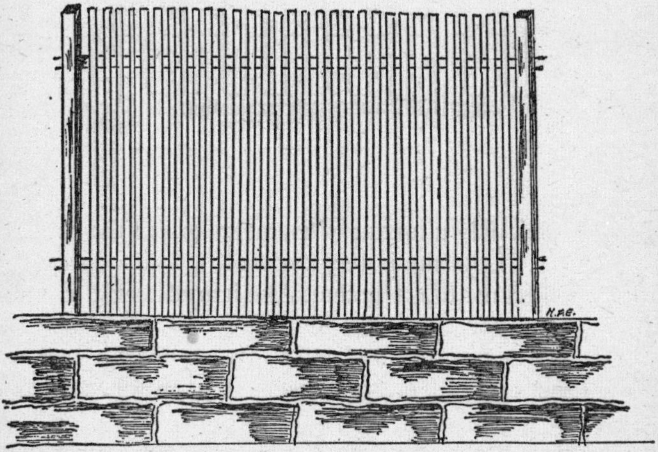

3. Slatted fencing using slats of 2 in. or less. Probably 1 in. vertical slats are aesthetically best.

to protect a flower bed or other desirable feature which is in view from the house, it may be advisable to have an easy means of erection and removal, so that they can be put in place at the first sign of a storm and removed when the danger is past.

One of the best ways to do this is to sink 2-in. land drains along the line you have decided to fence. These pipes should be spaced so as to accommodate the legs of the hurdles as illustrated below.

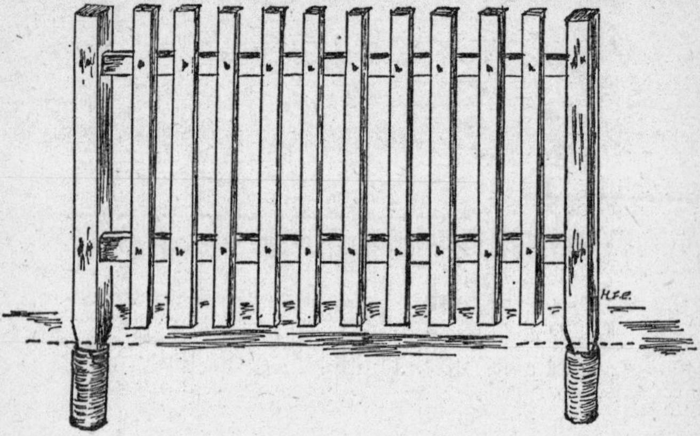

It is then only a matter of moments to slip the hurdles into place. If the site is very exposed, a wire loop can be made to lash the tops together. Also it is advisable to make a simple wooden plug for the top of each drain pipe, or they may become so full of soil and other débris when not in use that the rapid erection essential to this scheme is not possible.

Purpose-made slatted fences can of course be made. They look much more attractive and can be left in position for the whole winter if felt desirable.

Living Shelter for Summer

Summer storms are a perpetual hazard for all in windy places, and many plants in the garden need protection at this time, rather than in winter; the vegetable garden and summer annuals are common examples. Tall-growing plants of herbaceous habit are useful for such a purpose. Many a successful allotment in windy places owes its success to the Jerusalem artichoke. This very accommodating relative of the sunflower produces a tuber which can be bought like seed potatoes in the spring. Planted 4 to 6 in. deep in rows 2 ft 6 in. apart and with 15 in. between tubers, it will throw up stout stems up to 6 ft high. These are decidedly wind-hardy and make an excellent wind filter, with the added bonus of a winter root crop for consumption.

Save for keeping the weeds down with a hoe, they require little cultivation. Cut down the stalks in early winter. The tubers can be left in the ground and dug as required. Do not forget to reserve sufficient for the next season. Not everyone enjoys Jerusalem artichokes as a vegetable when eaten like turnips, etc, but few do not appreciate the wonderful soup made from them.

Runner beans can be used similarly if the household does not have to depend entirely on this perimeter row for all its supplies of beans. They should be regarded as an insurance policy. Frequently you will harvest a crop; occasionally the storms will claim them as victims, but the rest of the garden will benefit.

In the flower garden the use of temporary living shelter is rather in the form of a supplement and assistance to the real shelter borders rather than a major utility.

Low walls and hedges often have small areas of turbulence associated with them. If the source of trouble can be traced it is possible to help by putting in groups of plants such as the tall bearded irises, with their sword-shaped leaves, to act as a secondary filter. Groups of red-hot-poker (see Chapter 7) or the mallow (*Lavatera trimestris*) may also be used. I have always wondered at the amazing wind and salt tolerance of these attractive but not obviously sturdy plants.

Other non-shrubby plants which have merit in this way include:

Catananche caerulea
Clematis calycina
Echinops ritro
Eryngium amethystinum
Euphorbia wulfenii
Gynerium argenteum
Phormium tenax (New Zealand Flax)
Salvia superba
Sedum maximum atropurpureum
Stachys lanata (Lamb's Ear)
Venidio-arctotis grandis

Plants Protected by Nature

Most people who live at the seaside would be able to tell you, without knowing why, that grey foliage plants thrive exceptionally well in such places. It is because these plants, with some others, have made physical adjustments to their construction which enable them to withstand storm and spray.

If you examine the grey leaf of a plant such as *Senecio laxifolius* you will discover the greyness is caused by a covering of hairs. These can be rubbed off to display a green leaf below; the plant has a barrier to protect the working parts of the leaf from storm and spray. Many of the senecios have this covering of hairs or a felt-like lining to their undersides, as in *S. monroi*. See in Chapter 6.

Similarly the waxy coating which gives a grey bloom to the foliage of dianthus and similar plants is a protective adaptation.

Yet again we have plants, such as escallonias, which exude a sticky mucilage on their foliage which seems to serve the same purpose. Not all escallonias use this device, so it is necessary to know which are most efficient in this manner when planting in an exposed zone. Two of the best are *E. macrantha* and *E. rubra*. See in Chapter 3.

Other modifications Nature has devised to enable plants to withstand the worst weather include dispensation with leaves in the normal accepted form and the transfer of their duties of food manufacture to shoots which are of course much tougher. Gorse is an excellent example, closely followed by the tamarisk.

Another good plant which manages to survive by adapting its shoots to carry out the function of leaves is the Spanish gorse, *Genista hispanica.*

Some plants develop a specially tough outer layer of cells (epidermis) as in the case of the ubiquitous *Euonymus japonicus*; in this group too is the evergreen oak, *Quercus ilex* and that supremely good seashore plant the sea-buckthorn, *Hippophae rhamnoides.*

Another protective trick employed by plants is the doubling of the epidermis. The shrubby species of veronicas (*Hebe*) uses this device together with a very effective arrangement of its young leaves around the growing points. This enables the bud to develop behind successive pairs of leaves folded like hands in prayer. A few plants protect their buds (*Coprosma baueri*) by a viscid fluid not unlike that protecting the leaves of some escallonias.

The protection of the vital apical bud is a most important one. Many trees fail to make progress, even though they are in other respects relatively tough, through their inability to grow on after a storm because the leading bud has been killed. Time after time their young growth perishes in a storm resulting in stunted growth. It is this which causes the characteristic shorn-off appearance of any much exposed group of trees.

Zones of Protection

Bearing in mind these plant characteristics which can help us in our choice of suitable plants, there are three zones of planting which can be distinguished, subject to the size of one's property.

Outer Zone. This is the first line of defence and necessarily very exposed. Only the toughest plants are suitable and the species should be selected for that character rather than for beauty. The zone's width up to 30 ft should be as wide as available space allows. It is best mechanically cultivated; possibly by contract as it is sure to be difficult. If there are any existing plants – the odd willow, thorn, etc – do not disturb, but cultivate around them. A closely spaced chespale fence makes a good outer boundary; within this put your selected plants closely, so that they may protect each other. A 2 oz per square yard dressing of bone meal will help the plants away.

Middle Zone. As the Outer Zone plants will rarely achieve enough height to protect a garden, it is advisable, where there is room, to plant two or three rows of trees, preferably evergreen. These can be planted as seedlings or young plants 12–18 in. apart direct into the turf in rows 10 ft apart. Remove alternate plants as soon as they touch in the rows, until spaced for the full expected growth of the species, encouraging growth right down to ground level.

Inner Zone. These are the plants which provide the basic plantings for enjoyment within the shelter provided by the outer zones. A selection of the best trees and shrubs will be found in subsequent chapters.

PLANTS FOR THE OUTER ZONE

This is the first line of defence; here it is a battle for survival in which only those plants which have been adapted by nature during thousands of years of struggle in exposed places can hope to succeed.

One of the most rewarding ways of making a selection is to take a walk along the coastline near your garden to be. You will very soon begin to appreciate the particular plants which in the local soil, temperature and other climatic factors, make the most suitable protectors. Not all will be beautiful or desirable, but they will be tough and durable; therefore I advise you to use the best of these plants as the basis of your outer planting and do not be diverted by anything you may read here – or anywhere else – which sounds better.

We are looking for plants which, while living in these unpromising surroundings, will provide shelter throughout the year. It follows that a mixture including evergreens is needed. No great height is sought, up to say 5 to 6 ft; in a few cases, such as poplar, this can be induced by cutting back to near the ground periodically, thereby encouraging strong young basal growth. I regard the following as the best in this restricted category. Others are to be found in the chapter on hedges, which need special consideration.

Sea-buckthorn (*Hippophae rhamnoides*). Possibly the hardiest of all beside the sea. It will grow with its toes apparently in the sea and with nothing more nourishing than sand dunes to sustain it. The winter shape is somewhat gaunt but in summer it clothes its boughs in pleasant, narrow, grey leaves and in the female form festoons its boughs with attractive orange berries; these berries, unhappily, smell revoltingly of stale beer and stain badly anything with which they may come in contact. Altogether it is best enjoyed where it grows, for the boughs also bear ferocious thorns. The male and female flowers are borne on separate bushes, so if you wish to have berries a mixture must be planted say one male to five female. A few firms graft a piece of male on their female bushes for clients who want one only. It suckers freely and will form a thicket as unpleasantly impenetrable as any clump of gorse; ask any golfer at Burnham and Berrow Golf Course in Somerset, where it is a notable constituent of the rough. It will also make a hedge.

Tamarisk (*Tamarix*). The hardiest of these feathery,

frail-looking but actually supremely hardy shrubs are *Tamarix anglica* and *T. gallica*. For shelter purposes they are best pruned back to about one-third their height in June, after they have borne their foam of pink flowers in May. This prevents their becoming bare at the base and thus losing much of their utility as shelter. Other species are better in the more decorative parts of the garden (Chapter 6).

Sycamore (*Acer pseudo-platanus*). This common tree needs to be coppiced, i.e. cut back to near the ground so that young shoots break out. These, kept to 6 or 8 ft, are hardy even in the coldest and least hospitable places.

Willow. *Salix alba* and in particular the goat-willow, *S. caprea*, can be found making scrubby, wind-breaking growth on most coasts. Any foot-long shoot pushed into the ground at any season when the leaves are off the plants will root readily by the spring.

Sloe or Blackthorn (*Prunus spinosa*). A very slow-growing plant with a creeping root system which suckers freely – a distinct advantage in a shelter belt of this character. Its bleak and uncompromising outline is liberally strewn with vicious spines. Its flowers are white and pleasant enough, giving rise to tiny black plums which are usually called sloes. They are much beloved by the country wine-makers; sloe gin is perhaps the best known.

Elder (*Sambucus nigra*). A quick grower whose rapid growth and large leaves conceal its ability to survive equally the sea's full blast or a windswept moor. It is very much a countryman's plant – elderberry wine is one recipe from the extensive folklore of medicines and cordials believed by our forefathers to cure illness. One which is not a myth is an elderberry flower in a gooseberry pie to give a champagne flavour!

Box Thorn (*Lycium chinense*). No beauty this. Its multitude of thin, wiry arching branches will thrive in the most inhospitable spots, scrambling down a cliff or through other plants, bearing greyish leaves, insignificant starry purple flowers followed by orange red berries.

The above are the hardiest of the leaf dropping or deciduous species suitable to the Outer Zone. As shelter is also important in winter, it is advisable to add evergreens to the mixture. The following are good for this purpose.

Gorse (*Ulex europaeus*). One of the finest, as well as one of the most beautiful plants for resisting wind and salt spray. See Chapter 3.

Tree Purslane (*Atriplex halimus*). A sober, grey, and rather uninteresting plant, but with rare qualities of tough resistance. It seldom tops 5 ft, seems hardy anywhere in these islands, is quick growing and evergreen – if such a term can be applied to dusky silver-grey – is useful on dry sandy soils and is rapidly propagated by soft-wood cuttings in summer in sandy frames or by hard-wood cuttings in the open in autumn. Possibly this is the most satisfactory shrub for a quick-growing hedge behind which other plants may be established.

Euonymus japonicus. Where the climate suits, the best of the evergreens and a 'must' for any shelter belt. For its many virtues and occasional failings, see the chapter on hedges.

Privet (*Ligustrum vulgare*). This is the wild privet which you may find difficult to buy, but if you can get cuttings from the wild plants they root easily out of doors buried half their length and make a stronger, tougher, more evergreen plant than the commoner oval-leaved *L. ovalifolium*, which can be used if wild privet is unobtainable. See also Chapter 3.

Wire Netting Plant (*Muehlenbeckia complexa*). There are places in the Scilly Isles where this New Zealander seems the only plant capable of survival. It is a rampant climber, equally happy ascending a telegraph pole or submerging a wooden fence in an impenetrable thicket. Its growth consists of small, black, wiry stems, with tiny, often violin-shaped, leaves, though they vary in shape considerably.

It is utterly indifferent to the elements and makes a splendid windbreak on its own if allowed to grow through chespale or similar fencing or to submerge unwanted or less useful plants. It is not reliably hardy except in the south and west.

Olearia haastii. There are several of the New Zealand daisy bushes which can earn a place in our gardens but only this species and perhaps *O. albida* and *O. oleifolia* have proved themselves frost-hardy and impervious to salty winds. All are dingy grey and rather uninteresting.

Suckering plants. In general, species which sucker freely do well in bleak coastal areas. Even in the Orkneys the salmonberry, *Rubus spectabilis*, will produce low thickets of shelter, but be careful that it does not invade the garden proper. The white poplar, *Populus alba*, is another useful suckerer, as are also the willow and sea-buckthorn already mentioned.

MIDDLE ZONE PLANTS

The middle zone is usually composed of trees, since height is of importance. It cannot be too strongly emphasized that in making a choice your main guide should be species which are doing well in your own locality. You will find lists in this book and elsewhere of the best of those tolerant of windy places, but they must also be attuned to local climate and soil. Your own eyes will often be your best adviser.

It is not practicable to have a middle zone of this character unless you have plenty of room. At least one row (and much better three or four rows) of trees must be allowed to grow to their full height and width in so far as the wind will allow. Thus anything between 30 ft and 120 ft may be necessary. It will be found that the most exposed row will be shorn off and the succeeding rows progressively less so, and in this way the whole belt appears to lean away from the wind.

There is some merit in a mixed plantation of species. This avoids too solid a barrier that could have all the ill effects of a wall; it also allows for variety in growth height which increases the effectiveness of the barrier and ensures the probability that some, at any rate, of your choices are successful. This choice is the most difficult task. It should be composed partly of deciduous and partly of evergreen species. Of the former, the most wind-hardy are the sycamore (*Acer pseudo-platanus*), thorn (*Crataegus oxycantha*), wych elm (*Ulmus glabra*), Cornish elm (*U. carpinifolia* 'Cornubiensis'), Guernsey elm (*U. carpinifolia sarniensis*), black Italian poplar (*Populus serotina*), *P. robusta*, Swedish whitebeam (*Sorbus intermedia*) and the ash (*Fraxinus excelsior*) except on chalk.

The evergreens are rather more numerous and in some ways more useful. None are better, once they have grown, than the evergreen- or holm-oak (*Quercus ilex*). It is most remarkably tough and in many places can be found succeeding right down to the shore but does take up to ten years to reach a useful height. In contrast, a very quick-growing species is *Cupressus macrocarpa*, the Monterey cypress. It is not a plant for very cold areas but it is cheap, it must be planted young and from pots and its fragrant green foliage should not be cut. In these circumstances it will grow rapidly in most mild but windy places. Rapidly rivalling it in popularity and more wind-hardy than the Monterey cypress is the more expensive hybrid *x Cupressocyparis leylandii*, the Leyland cypress, which I discuss in the chapter on hedges.

Of the more widely spreading conifers, the most valuable are the pines. Anyone who has been to the wonderful Dorien-Smith garden on Tresco, in the Scilly Isles, will be conscious that it could not have succeeded without the sheltering fringe of *Pinus radiata*, the Monterey pine. It is a plant for the milder coastal regions and is a most handsome tree bearing bright green, densely crowded leaves. Like the Monterey cypress, it needs planting young and from pots. It will grow rapidly to form a belt of what is perhaps the loveliest of the pines.

Another beautiful pine for the milder parts is the Bishop pine (*P. muricata*). It is a picturesque tree forming a dense rather flat head of blue-green foliage. It is reasonably hardy and certainly not slow growing. It will not succeed on chalky soil.

The maritime pine, *P. pinaster*, is a much-planted species for sandy coastal districts – Bournemouth for example. It is reliable but somewhat ungainly.

The Austrian pine, *P. nigra austriaca*, is perhaps the best all-rounder. A broad-headed, densely branched, dark-foliaged tree, it thrives better than any other pine in chalky soils and in bleak exposures, even near the sea. With age it does tend to become thin at the base and needs the help of the Outer Zone plants.

A near relative, the Corsican pine, *P. nigra calabrica*, is well nigh as accommodating save that it is not very happy on chalk or on very exposed places. It is an especially bad transplanter and must be moved when 6 to 12 in. high.

Other possibilities are the mountain pine, *P. mugo*, more of a bush than a tree, which succeeds in almost all soils and exposures. One of the very few really lime-tolerant pines is the black pine of Japan, *P. thunbergii*. It thrives in poor soils. It is unusual and most attractive in having light yellow-brown branches and elongated, white winter buds.

Stabilizing Sand, Shingle and Cliffs

The need for stabilizing the raw faces of nature lies in a desire to see that erosion by water or wind does not occur or the gardener right on the seashore may be faced by tough problems. Water erosion can arise from wave action physically scouring away the beach or cliff face; or it may be from surface drainage where there is a rapid run-off from the surface after a heavy storm or at lower levels where the water, on soaking in, strikes a layer of clay or rock. Erosion by wind occurs when the force of the wind picks up particles of sand, even large grit, and uses it to batter whatever is in its path.

One of the effective ways of reducing these destructive forces in really difficult places is to establish such a successful root system among the loose surfaces that there is a considerable resistance to movement.

In Sand. In some respects this is the most difficult problem as it is all too easy for the first high wind to bury any plantings you may do. A lateral, low fence of brushwood is very valuable to assist in this. In planting sand dunes you cannot do better than use the species which naturally grow in your district in such places. It is likely to be mainly grasses from the following list:

Couch grass (*Agropyron repens, A. junceiforme*)
Sea lyme grass (*Elymus arenarius*)
Sea barley (*Hordeum marinum*)
Marram grass (*Ammophila arenaria*)
Sand cat's-tail (*Phleum arenarium*)
Red fescue grass (*Festuca rubra*)

These can be planted in small clumps 2 ft apart. In suitable places unrooted cuttings a foot long of tamarisk or the small hardier willows such as *Salix caprea* or *repens* can be pushed in to half their depth. They will frequently root.

Mud. Where this is a problem, the cord-grasses, *Spartina maritima* and *S.* × *townsendii*, are outstanding. So is the sea-aster (*A. tripolium*); other native plants to encourage are the glasswort (*Salicornia perennis*), the club-rush (*Scirpus maritimus*) and the glass-wrack (*Zostera marina*).

Shingle. One might well imagine it impossible to establish plants on a depth of rounded stones containing no observable form of plant food, but, in fact, a number of deep-rooted, often fleshy-leaved, indigenous plants do quite well. Sea-kale (*Crambe maritima*), sea-beet (*Beta maritima*), sea-campion (*Silene maritima*), sea-pea (*Lathyrus japonicus*), horned-poppy (*Glaucium flavum*), and some grasses, mainly those named as good in sand, and the black-bent (*Agrostis gigantea*) are among the commonest.

On Cliff faces. Obviously a tremendously variable problem. For present purposes I am assuming the engineering problems of securing an angle of repose of one foot in three or better has been solved and that a certain amount of soil and humus have been secured.

It is important that small plants are used in any planting project. Most of those named earlier for the outer defences are suitable. Gorse, as exemplified on Cornish cliffs and in Guernsey, is very successful. Tamarisk, box-thorn, elder, blackthorn, goat-willow, sea-purslane, are also among the hardiest. There is another way of dealing with cliff faces and I am indebted to my colleague, Mr E. W. B. Gale of Poole, Dorset, for the following:

'A very effective form of stabilizing a cliff face or steep bank is by covering the whole area with heather clots. It is appreciated that this is only possible in certain districts. The heather "clots" are cut 9 in. square, with a depth of 5–6 in. of peaty soil attached, and are laid closely on the prepared face. It will be necessary to peg certain sections securely to prevent any possible slipping, using pegs of willow or poplar, which I previously mentioned may root. Needless to say, work should commence at the base of the cliff, and the heather clots top dressed with screened soil to fill in the interstices.

'In some instances it is possible to leave small pockets for planting shrubs, such as *Senecio rotundifolius*, *S. monroi*, gorse, or many other of the shrubs which have been previously recommended. In some instances, where there is a certain amount of sand movement, one can attempt to stabilize the sand by using marram grass (*Ammophila arenaria*) or red fescue (*Festuca rubra*) and its variety *F. rubra arenaria*. These must be planted in clumps and it must be stated that the conditions which make for success in growing these grasses should really be avoided, that is, a fairly good supply of sand in which to root upwards.

'Other useful shrubs which are worth a trial are the common ivy (*Hedera helix*) and in the South and Westwards, the Hottentot-fig (*Mesembryanthemum edule*). This plant in the Poole and Bournemouth areas has survived many years, but is severely damaged by frosts on occasion. Just a little further inland, two shrubs which are worth planting on steep sloping banks are the rose-of-sharon (*Hypericum calycinum*) and *Gaultheria shallon*. The latter requires a neutral soil.'

Chapter 3

HEDGES

INTRODUCTION – TALL FORMAL HEDGES – SHORT FORMAL ONES – INFORMAL – CULTURAL GUIDE SERIES

Here we come to a special form of protection that needs a chapter to itself.

A hedge is a living fence which may mark the boundary of one's property or provide divisions within it. It can be formal, which really means capable of being clipped, or informal, when free growth, bearing flowers in due season, is desired.

The choice of hedges is very wide, bearing in mind the necessity of the basic shelter discussed earlier, but they should not be regarded as merely a garden utility. They are capable of being objects of beauty in their own right and may greatly enhance the garden's charm. Nothing surpasses the quiet, restful green of a well-clipped yew hedge – the perfect foil for colour. Scarlet salvias and golden violas are a somewhat brash mixture alone, but place them against the sheer, clipped, dark green of a yew hedge and they acquire a dignity and charm that one had not appreciated before. Quite different is the rôle of an informal hedge of a multiflora rose such as 'Queen Elizabeth'. About 5 ft high and smothered in pink for many months, it is a sheer delight.

Perhaps the fact that neither of these examples is suited to an exposed place in the seaside garden will emphasize the importance of choice of subject in this context. Where it is desired to have a boundary hedge which will have to bear the full brunt of anything the elements may choose to throw at it, then the choice is limited to those plants already discussed for the Outer Zone. A reference to the most suitable hedge plants will be found there.

At the other end of the exposure scale lie those parts of the garden which have no problems more exacting than those in a garden inland. For these unexposed places we may select freely from the following lists, which are far from exhaustive.

FORMAL OR CLIPPED HEDGES FOR UNEXPOSED POSITIONS:

Carpinus betulus (Hornbeam)
Chamaecyparis lawsoniana (Lawson's Cypress)
× *Cupressocyparis leylandii* (Leyland's Cypress)
Fagus sylvatica (Beech)
Ilex species (Holly)
Laurus nobilis (Bay)
Laurus nobilis 'Angustifolia' (Willow-leaf Bay)
Lavendula spica and its cultivars (Lavender)
Lonciera nitida
Pittosporum tenuifolium (Mild areas only)
Prunus laurocerasus (Laurel)
Taxus baccata (Yew)
Thuya plicata

INFORMAL OR FREE-GROWING HEDGES FOR UNEXPOSED PLACES:

Berberis darwinii (Barbery)
Berberis × *stenophylla* (Barbery)
Choisya ternata (Mexican-orange-blossom)
Forsythia × *intermedia* 'Spectabilis'
Fuchsia magellanica 'Riccartonii'

Hydrangea macrophylla and its cultivars
Olearia macrodonta
Philadelphus species and cultivars (Mock-orange)
Pseudosasa japonica (Bamboo)
Roses, free-growing species and cultivars, *eg* Penzance briars
Rosmarinus officinalis (Rosemary)
Sinarundinaria nitida (Bamboo)
Skimmia japonica
Symphoricarpus laevigatus 'White Hedge' (Snowberry)
Syringa vulgaris and its cultivars (Lilac)
Viburnum tinus (Laurustinus)

Between these two groups of hedges are others which more specifically answer the special hedge problems of the seaside garden; that is to say, those which will accept some spray but not too much, will filter the wind with a little scorching but will soon repair, withstand the hardest frosts likely to be experienced in the district and will add beauty as well as utility to the garden scene. Such a list would be very long and contain many only suited to the milder west coast; I therefore propose to discuss only a few of the very best, noting their hardiness.

The first requirement is that the planter of a new hedge should decide what he is planting for. Is it to shield his garden from the wind or from the eyes of his neighbours? Does he want it to flower? Is it to be evergreen or does it not matter if its leaves fall for the winter? Or is it to divide his own garden so that one feature is distinct from another?

Having answered honestly to himself, he can now choose the plant which appeals to him as the most desirable solution and subject the choice to a further sieve. Will it grow on my soil? For to plant a screen of, say, camellia or rhododendron on limy soils, which they hate, would be futile. Will it grow in my district? The delightful evergreen *Griselinia littoralis* would not survive long in the low temperatures of the east coast. Is my district's rainfall and temperature too *high*? *Euonymus japonicus*, the evergreen par excellence from Yarmouth to Torquay, is not a success in Cornwall, because the very long, soft growths it makes are so tender they are killed in the first cold snap.

As six feet is usually tall enough for an internal hedge, we will divide our list into groups above and below that figure; we will divide again into formal clipped hedges and those which are kept in trim by the occasional use of secateurs, *ie* the informal.

Tall Formal Hedges

Leyland's cypress. Among the evergreens the formidably-named × *Cupressocyparis leylandii* universally known as 'Leylandii' to the nurseryman and gardener, stands supreme. Its virtues make a formidable catalogue. It is the fastest-growing conifer we have, is quite hardy and I have not heard of any district in which it will not grow; it will stand clipping very well, is a pleasant bright green, and does not blow over in strong winds. Even on a very thin poor soil over chalk it will grow 12–18 in. in a year. As a free-growing specimen it forms a dense column. It is liable, however, to be scorched by heavily salt-laden gales.

Leyland's cypress is the child of a chance cross between *Chamaecyparis nootkatensis* and *Cupressus macrocarpa* – neither to be sneezed at as hedging plants in their own right. Although this cross happened towards the end of the last century it is only in the last twenty years that it has become commercially available. I imagine this was due to the great difficulty there was in propagating it before the advent of mist propagation. Plant them 2 ft 6 in. apart in a single row and keep the ground clean around the plants until growing freely. There are cheaper plants, but it is doubtful if any are better value. Do not forget it is a big tree – 50 feet or more in time – so restrict it firmly by clipping when it has reached a convenient height.

Escallonia. My experiences with trying to have my horticultural cake and eat it have not been very successful. A doubled-edged pruning saw sounds a good idea until one finds that in removing the unwanted branch with one edge, the other is merrily cutting into parts which should remain. So, in recommending the escallonia as an evergreen hedge which will stand clipping and yet give a good show of flower, we find the exception to prove the rule, for it is truly so.

Escallonia hedges are best trimmed in August; they will then make short new growths before winter sets in which in the following early summer produces a most attractive display.

Escallonias produce a gummy layer over their leaves which seems to protect the vital tissues from wind and salt; the large-leaved species seem to do this most freely and accordingly are usually the best for protection. *E. macrantha* and *E. rubra* are typical.

Asked to name the toughest of all most knowledgeable people would, I think, choose *E. macrantha*. It will make up a 10 ft hedge, bearing rosy-crimson flowers set in glossy dark green foliage. *E. rubra* bears pink flowers and is more frost-hardy than *E. macrantha*, so should be preferred in colder parts.

If you seek a minimum of trimming, you may well use those fastigiate or erect-growing varieties, *E.* 'Red Hedger' or *E.* 'Crimson Spire'. The latter will grow 18 in. each year when happy and can be highly recommended. Lastly, if a 5 ft hedge will suffice, try *E.* 'William Watson'. It makes exceptionally compact growth, has pleasant red flowers which bespangle it for several months. See also Chapter 6.

Euonymus japonicus, the Japanese spindle-tree, is the doyen of seaside hedges where it is not too mild (Channel Isles, Cornwall, etc) or too cold (north of Birmingham save extreme west). This is a really handsome plant when well grown on good soil and still young. It has suffered somewhat from its own virtues. It will grow even in poor soil, in great exposure, untended and unfed; consequently it can be seen eking out an existence in many a dingy garden neglected by man, crippled with mildew and with aphis but still alive and green when all else has long since given up the struggle. This is not its true image; it is a bright, glossy-leaved evergreen as cheerful as any you may find. You will rarely find it flowering. I have only seen it so doing on the cliff face at Brighton where plants set out in 1882 are some 60 ft high and regrettably showing signs that their allotted span in approaching. Here upon a day in October or November you may find the sprays of golden fruits; each capsule will open to show orange-scarlet seeds on a golden backcloth. Attractive, but you are unlikely to see it on a garden hedge.

Another of its virtues is its ability to withstand moving at an advanced age. I once advised against trying to move a 50-year-old euonymus hedge: the owner quite correctly thought he knew better, moved it, kept it well fed and waterered and today, five years later, it is still a thriving hedge in his garden.

One of the unexpected facts to arise from that most interesting investigation into the behaviour of plants for shelter, carried out at the Ministry of Agriculture Experimental Horticulture Station at Rosewarne in Cornwall, was the discovery that *Euonymus japonicus*, so excellent in apparently less hospitable climes, was not hardy here in high rainfall and little severe frost. It seems that the mild autumns cause excessively exuberant growth which succumbs to the subsequent frosts to an extent which removes it from the first line shrubs in such very mild areas.

The Japanese spindle-tree is easily propagated by summer cuttings in a close cold frame.

Beech (*Fagus sylvatica*) and **Hornbeam** (*Carpinus betulus*). Good deciduous hedges in this group are not common. Probably the best of all are these two; the practical difference between them in so far as making a hedge is concerned is negligible. It has been said that one or other is better able to retain its golden brown autumn tinted foliage throughout the winter. Both seem to do this equally satisfactorily to me if clipping is done at the correct time, *ie* July/August, so that the short young growths which follow have a chance to harden a little and bear full-sized leaves before the autumn. Thus they will carry their russet cloak through till the young green flush appears in the spring.

Beech is not hardy to frost when young, so needs a little protection if planted on a frosty site. Once over this phase of youth, it is as hardy as the next hedge and may make a hedge or screen of great height, up to 50 ft if required. Some of our finest and tallest hedges are of beech – at Blairgowrie in Perthshire, at Levens Hall in Westmorland, and many others.

An idea you may like to consider is the 'Tartan' mixture hedge sometimes planted. This is mainly beech or hornbeam with an occasional evergreen oak, copper or purple beech. It is most attractive and an unusual effect is produced. You can see one in that lovely National Trust Garden at Hidcote in Gloucestershire.

Short Formal Hedges

Lonicera nitida will make a most useful 'soft' hedge up to 5 ft. It is cheap, clips well, is hardy save in the severest spots, grows quickly and is a pleasant green. But it needs several clippings a year to retain even growth, can be damaged by snow and it is not long lived. *Lonicera pileata yunnanensis* is better but not easily obtained.

Hebe speciosa (*Veronica speciosa*) is a New Zealand plant and is not hardy in frosts of more than 15–20°F, so every few years one has to face a replanting. Treated as an informal hedge it will make 4 ft high by as much through and is rarely without its clusters of dark blue flowers. Summer cuttings in a cold frame are a useful insurance against heavy frost. See also Chapter 6.

For a grey hedge that is more of a short division wall, rather than a screen for shelter, **lavender** (*Lavandula spica*) is perhaps the most prized of all. Its fragrant, dusty-blue spikes associate superbly with pink flowers, especially roses, and with *Lilium regale.* If height is desirable the tallest cultivar is 'Grappenhall'. For dwarfer purposes use 'Twickle Purple' or, shorter still, 'Hidcote'. Clip hard each year to avoid straggly growth and keep it compact.

This seems an appropriate place to say something about **Privet** (*Ligustrum ovalifolium*), a semi-evergreen, and about ***Crataegus monogyna,*** whose common names are legion, among them being 'quick', 'hawthorn', and 'may'. These are the commonest of all hedging plants and the cheapest, so readers may properly ask why more expensive plants seem to be the main ones recommended. Let us be quite clear these are two superb hedging plants. They have almost all the virtues, they stand clipping well; they are cheap, well tended they look well, they are not particular as to soil, they withstand the onslaughts of children and of animals, they are hardy and reasonably long lived. But they have been so widely planted that one cannot feel that one's garden achieves any additional distinction as a result of their choice, but if this is not a factor in your mind and a utilitarian, straightforward, protective device is your objective then you need look no further.

Privet has one widely acknowledged fault. It is a gross feeder and will impoverish the ground up to 4 ft from its edge. There is a pleasant golden form *Ligustrum ovalifolium* 'Aureo-marginatum' which makes a good hedge and might well be more frequently used unpruned as a colour contrast shrub in borders.

Informal Hedges

One of the prerequisites of the decision to plant an informal hedge is that there should be room to grow it. This frequently means you must have as much width as the anticipated height. If you have not, it means trimming the sides to a straight line and you end up with a formal hedge.

The **daisy-bush** or *Olearia macrodonta* 'Major' is a good example. It makes a really magnificent evergreen hedge in the milder parts such as the Isle of Man, West of Scotland, etc. It will easily top 12 ft in such places but can be kept down by judicious pruning of the leading shoots. It certainly can be the same distance through. This good plant has broad, greyish, holly-like leaves and in June the bushes are entirely covered with clusters of white flowers; I remember smelling musk in the garden at home as a very small child; today musk is scentless but this olearia has that same scent as I remember it. *Olearia macrodonta* 'Minor' is smaller in all its parts, but still makes a satisfactory hedge up to 6 or 7 ft.

Perhaps the most widely planted evergreen informal hedge is **Berberis stenophylla,** rightly so, as this plant comes near to being the best of all evergreen shrubs. Quite hardy, it will form a dense hedge up to 10 ft high, out of which are thrown slender, arching sprays up to a couple of feet long, dressed in small, narrow leaves. These shoots are wreathed each April with small, rich, golden flowers. It flourishes in clay, sand, or chalk. There are some good dwarf clones, such as 'Irwinii' and 'Coccinea'. All are difficult to move and are best planted from pots.

One of the parents of this plant is *B. darwinii.* It makes a superb informal hedge in its own right. It is of much stiffer habit, has shining dark green leaves about 1 in. long, profuse in richest orange-yellow bloom and is often laden with plum-coloured berries in autumn.

We do not often see hedges of **gorse,** yet, as that great nurseryman and supreme plantsman, Harold Hillier, has said so truly:

'If our native gorses were rare exotics they would be sought alike by connoisseur and garden designer. It would be impossible to imagine in any landscape a richer mass of chrome yellow, intermixed with the occasional splash of deep lemon yellow, than one sees covering the downs around Slieve Donard in Northern Ireland in April. This is *Ulex. europaeus.* In August and September, as one approaches central Wales from Herefordshire, the countryside is enriched with lower growing masses of *U. gallii.* Many have roved those lovely downs which rise from Salcombe harbour in South Devon which in late summer becomes a patchwork quilt of golden gorse and purple heather. In parts of the New Forest we meet *U. nanus,* our third native species, which also flowers in the autumn with the heather and only attains half the size of *U. europaeus.*'

One of my own abiding memories is of a golden glory of gorse clothing the shelving cliffs of Guernsey against a background of the blue sea beyond. It is rarely without blossom, hence the saying 'When gorse is out of bloom, kissing's out of season'. Its early flowers offer a rich bee pasture. It has a scent of honey and almond which hangs on the air in good weather, so as to become linked in one's scent memory with warmth and high summer and hay making.

Gorse is not completely hardy in this country but seems

to be rarely killed outright, even in a winter like 1963, but it may suffer from severe scorching winds inland.

In making a hedge, the double gorse, *U. europaeus* 'Plenus' is the best form, indeed it is the best anywhere in the garden as opposed to the shelter belt, though it does not set seed as the single-flowered does freely. I have heard good reports of, but have not personally seen a cultivar *U. europaeus* 'Scilly Gold', which is a deep golden-orange and which makes a slightly taller hedge of 5–6 ft. Although you may often see gorse growing in poor, dry soils, it is best to give it as good a start as any other by thorough preparation of the trench; many books misguide one here. Plant out from pots, as it greatly resents root disturbance. Two feet apart will be near enough if you keep the ground clear between the plants until they are growing strongly, where they will make a devastating barrier against man and beast.

Turning to the shorter deciduous hedges, I have a great regard for a **lilac,** *Syringa palibiniana*, which is also known as *S. velutina*. You may see a hedge of this outside the laboratories at the Royal Horticultural Society's garden at Wisley. In time it will reach 5–6 ft but it is slow growing and has the great merit of flowering profusely from a tender age. It can, in fact, have a home on the rock garden for a year or two. But do not imagine a large, heavy truss of flowers like the ordinary lilac, for *S. palibiniana* bears quite frail clusters of lilac or lilac-pink colour and is sweetly fragrant. When not in flower it still retains an attractive shape. With pruning you can retain it to any desired size.

In milder districts one cannot ignore the claims of the **fuchsia.** Since robustness is a most desirable quality, I think choice can be confined to the magnificent *Fuchsia magellanica* 'Riccartonii', which I describe in Chapter 6. Another possibility is the white *F.m.* 'Alba', which grows somewhat quicker. If you do take a chance for the sake of their beauty with these fuchsias, you must be prepared for the frost to cut them back to ground level. Leave last year's shoots on until danger of heavy frost has gone, as they are a slight protection. Then cut right back to the young growths that you will by then see appearing. In autumn in such districts a covering of bracken, coarse ashes etc, will help to protect the vital crown.

Spiraeas are not frequently seen as hedges, possibly because they are in no way suited to clipping, but as an informal division they have much to commend them. Among the most suitable are *Spiraea* × *arguta*, the 'foam of May', considered by many the finest of the white flowered spiraeas, and the rather taller *S.* × *vanhouttei*. The former flowers in April and May, the latter about a month later. These flowers are produced on graceful arching sprays of wood produced during the previous year. The flowers are freely clustered on the upper side of these shoots, weighing down the slender fronds with their profusion. As they flower on wood produced in the previous year, they benefit from having some of the older wood pruned out immediately after flowering. This encourages food supplies to the young growths which will be the flower bearing wood in the succeeding spring.

It is impossible to consider seaside hedges without considering the **hydrangea.** This genus is dealt with elsewhere, but in this context it is likely that *Hydrangea hortensia* 'Joseph Banks' is the one upon which one's choice should fall. It is doubtful whether it is worth planting away from the edge of the sea but where it can smell the salt breezes it is a superb plant, although the buds are not absolutely frost-hardy. The oldest variety grown in this country (for it was introduced by Sir Joseph Banks in 1789), it makes a hedge 5 ft high or more and adorns the end of every shoot with a large cream head which gradually turns pink and so to an assortment of those recessive complementary shades so beloved of the flower arranger. For other hydrangeas, see Chapter 6.

Finally, an indispensable evergreen for the seaside, ***Senecio laxifolius***. A truly handsome plant, up to 5 ft high when happy, which seems to be everywhere save the very bleakest coasts. It has grey foliage – silvery is not an exaggeration – which doubtless enables it to stand up to the fury of the sea. Its full glory is in June when cluster upon cluster of its delightful, golden daisy-like flowers burst open in a dazzling display. It is not a long-lived plant. It is advisable to start again every ten years or so.

Cultural Guide-Lines

The following condensed notes on the culture of hedges in general will, I hope, be a helpful guide.

REQUIREMENTS	REASONS
The Plant	
1. Should be bushy and short-jointed with a good fibrous root system.	1. Gives a well furnished hedge at near ground level. Fibrous roots make for easy transplanting.
2. Make sure roots are firm and moist.	2. Indicates good health before planting.
3. Trim all damaged roots with knife or secateurs before planting.	3. Prevents possible die-back and disease.
Planting times	
1. Deciduous hedges – October to March.	1. When sap is not rising and plant is dormant.
2. Evergreens – April to May.	2. When root system is most active and danger of winter gale desiccation is over.

REQUIREMENTS	REASONS
Planting distances	
1. Double hedge: 18–24 in. apart, staggered.	1. Only used where site is exposed and immediate protection is needed.
2. Single hedge: 9–18 in.	2. Nearly always adequate. Spacing depends upon size of plants and position.
Planting	
1. Use a line for marking edge of trench. Peg-out around curves.	1. Hedge must be straight when planted or follow a well-shaped curve if on a bend.
2. Take out a trench up to 2 ft wide and 2 ft deep.	2. Allows for full spread of roots when planting.
3. Fork manure or compost into bottom of trench and add up to 4 oz bonemeal or hoof-and-horn meal per yard run. Turf, where present should be chopped up and laid face-down in bottom of trench.	3. Gives a good start and quick growth. Fertilizer gives a better balance to growth, which should not be soft.
4. Do not plant for at least two weeks after digging.	4. Allows for settlement of soil.
5. Plant down centre of trench. Spread roots evenly, shake while planting and firm well.	5. Plants evenly spaced and level, with soil in close contact with roots, should quickly become established.
6. When planted, the shrubs should be at the same soil level as growing in the nursery before transplanting.	6. Ensures that hedge is firm, no roots exposed, stem not buried.

REQUIREMENTS	REASONS
After-care	
1. Cut back all main shoots as indicated in the pruning tables in Chapter 4.	1. This encourages production of a good bushy base to the hedge. If a leader is allowed to develop, the hedge will be very poorly furnished near the base. Makes a neat finish to the job.
2. Keep all weeds regularly controlled.	2. Weeds compete for food, encourage pests, and causc death of lower branches of hedge by cutting off light.
3. Cut regularly, gradually trimming to desired shape. Always ensure bottom of hedge is wider than top.	3. Encourages bushy growth and prevents formation of undesirable leaders. Fast-growing hedges may require cutting every eight weeks in summer to retain bushy growth. Slow-growing hedges, such as holly, need trimming once in August or September.
4. If weather after planting is dry, water well (2/3 gallons per square yard) and if possible give a mulch of compost, etc, especially to evergreens.	4. Helps prevent excessive transpiration and ensures that plant has a good start.
5. Replace any dead or diseased plants as soon as possible.	5. Ensures that hedge will have no gaps and that plants appear well matched in size.

Chapter 4

SAFEGUARDING THE GARDEN

PLANTING – STAKING – PRUNING

However well the garden may be protected, its success depends on the choice of living material and upon their growing healthily when planted. This is particularly true of shrubs and trees, with which I am concerned in this chapter.

Planting

All too often we are told that late autumn is the recommended time for planting shrubs, before the soil temperature drops. This is true for the deciduous ones, but just for a moment consider the conditions the poor evergreen must withstand if near to the sea or, indeed, in any exposed spot. More than likely, there will be six months of intermittent, climatic chaos. During every gale desiccation from high winds will be considerable and many an evergreen will die under such treatment before spring. It is much better to make these plantings in late April.

Of course, this means using pot-grown plants and adequate measures to see that they don't dry out. Planting positions should be prepared before the dry weather of the spring sets in. It is a fairly well accepted meteorological fact that March and April are dry months. Therefore it is helpful to dig out suitable holes amply big enough to take the roots of the plants you anticipate buying. Moist, shredded peat, together with a complete fertilizer, should be mixed with the soil excavated from the hole. The mixture should then be replaced until planting time a few weeks later.

If it is dryish at planting time the excavated soil must be re-moistened. Plant firmly, using the full weight of the planter, so that when finished there is a slight depression around the plant. Flood this and as soon as the water has soaked in rake dry soil round the plants to preserve a mulch, to which you can add rotten manure or garden refuse, freshly cut bracken shoots, or anything which is available to retain the moisture which has been so carefully introduced. Plants treated in this way withstand a prolonged dry spell and will certainly do far better than those that take their chance with autumn planting.

There is a good case to be made for lavish planting in exposed places; plant closely in threes and fives, or multiples thereof, rather than single plants. These groups quickly interlock to form one dense bush, and as such, are proof against the worst that the gales may do. Additionally, of course, there is less upkeep, as such dense growth keeps down weeds.

In a busy spring there is great temptation to neglect these simple rules for seaside planting. Please don't, for the most careful plant selection is a waste of time if the plants do not grow.

Staking

A very necessary adjunct to planting in exposed places. Stakes are not pretty things; they add nothing to the beauty of plant or garden, but they are the antidote to the rocking to and fro in the wind which brings death or poor growth to so many plants. A normal large shrub or tree has roots for two purposes – one to supply food, the other for anchorage. In the case of a newly-planted tree virtually no anchorage can be supplied until new root growth marries the existing root system with its new soil environment. The stake takes the place of those anchor roots for a year or two and prevents that disastrous rocking, which can have the effect of tearing of the feeding roots, so depriving it of food and water at a vital time.

Pruning

I put this in potted form and hope you will find it as good as any other.

OBJECT	REASON
1. To alter the natural shape.	1. Many objects, *eg* to allow people to walk under trees that may be grown with a 6–8 ft trunk bare of branches; or for topiary, *ie* the clipping of bushes to shapes – peacocks, etc; or just to get by.
2. To encourage new growth.	2. By cutting back an elderly growth, dormant buds will give rise to new shoots. These frequently flower better than older growths.
3. To remove dead, diseased, or wispy thin growths.	3. Preserves health, checks spread of decay and directs energy to wanted parts.
4. To reduce leaf area of freshly planted shrubs, especially evergreens.	4. Balances root system damaged in transplanting with leaf system.
5. To increase display of flowers by encouraging the growth of those shoots most likely to flower. The commonest form of pruning practised.	5. Because many shrubs flower best on growths less than a year old it is best to prune these immediately the flowers fade, *eg* forsythia in April.

GENERAL PRUNING GUIDE

If the shrub is not mentioned below it probably requires little pruning other than the removal of straggling growth.

Prune in March. Cut back laterals to 2–3 in. of previous year's growth:

Buddleia davidii
Ceanothus ('Gloire de Versailles' or deciduous type)
Cornus (coloured bark)
Hydrangea paniculata
Sambucus (Elder)
Spartium
Spiraea × *bumalda* 'Anthony Waterer'
Stephanandra (coloured bark)
Tamarisk
Willow (coloured bark)

Prune lightly immediately after flowering. Little pruning is required for the following shrubs, but individual branches, if straggling, should be cut out *completely*:

Abelia
Almond
Azara
Calycanthus (Allspice)
Camellia
Ceanothus, evergreen sorts
Chionanthus
Cistus
Crataegus (Thorns)
Garrya elliptica
Hamamelis
Laurustinus
Leptospermum
Pernettya

Little pruning needed for the following, but if the shrubs are straggling, they may safely be cut back:

Berberis
Chaenomeles speciosa
Chimonanthus (Winter Sweet)

Coronilla
Escallonia
Gorse
Kerria
Lilac
Malus (Crabs)
Ribes (Flowering Currant)
Spiraea × arguta
Spiraea thunbergii

Prune hard immediately after flowering.

Rubus (decorative brambles) – Treat like raspberry; cut down to the ground each year.

Thin out and cut back the shoots which have flowered to within a few inches of the old wood each year of the following:

Deutzia
Diervilla (Weigela)
Forsythia
Honeysuckle
Hydrangea macrophylla
Philadelphus

Prune the following strong-growing species annually to keep them within bounds, but they must not be cut back into the old hard wood:

Brooms (*Cytisus* and *Genista*).

Chapter 5

A SELECTION OF SMALL TREES

Since the moderating influence of the sea on temperature, enables tender trees and shrubs to be grown successfully, especially on the western coast where this is accentuated by the warm waters of the Gulf Stream, a complete list of the trees one could grow would list everything as hardy or near hardy in nursery catalogues. But it is necessary to bear in mind that at the seaside, tall trees are a hostage to fate, in that they are liable to grow up beyond the sheltering influence of the protective plantings. It seems prudent, therefore, to limit one's choice to those which have no great stature and so tend to keep their heads down naturally.

The succeeding list of small trees I consider worthy of a place in any garden of sufficient size for their individual beauty of flower or form. It is hoped that the reader, in using this chapter and the succeeding one on shrubs, will have in his other hand the catalogue of a good nurseryman and that what he reads here will act as a guide to the bewildering number of plants he will find offered for selection. It may well be over 2,000.

Acer. The maples are an enormous, hardy, and very beautiful family; most are easily cultivated, asking only a moderate supply of good soil and moisture.

They contain the well known Japanese maples, of which there are at least twenty varieties, most of them worth planting for their elegant form and beauty of leaf, as typified by *A. palmatum*. Particularly good clones of this species are the bronzy-crimson 'Atropurpureum', the coral-bark maple, 'Senkaki', which has its young shoots clothed in a rich coral red bark, and 'Osakazuki', whose fiery red autumnal colour is second to none.

Among the Japanese maples I also like *A. japonicum* for its clean, soft, green foliage, contrasting most effectively with the above. Its clones 'Aconitifolium' and 'Aureum' can be recommended.

Another group contains those whose especial attraction is their bark, particularly in winter. One might very well claim that *A. griseum*, the paper-bark maple from China, is one of the most attractive of all small trees. As the tree grows it splits off its bark in curling flakes of chestnut brown to reveal a polished orange-brown trunk below. In a shaft of winter sunshine, attractive indeed. Its branching is light and elegant, clothed in bluntly trifoliate, darkish green leaves which end the season in a glory of red or orange before falling to reveal the distinctive and unusual bark pattern to cheer us through the depths of winter. Definitely a good buy.

A. davidii and *A. pennsylvanicum*, the snake-bark maple, are others with distinctive bark patterns. My personal favourite has the difficult name *A. grosseri* var. *hersii*, which has a magnificently marbled bark, fine autumn colour and chains of conspicuous, pendulous fruits.

An American tree which used to be very much more popular than it now is, is the box-elder, *Acer negundo*. The type is rather dull but 'Variegatum' bears leaves which are so conspicuously bordered with white – or indeed may be wholly white – that it becomes a noteworthy feature of the garden, the more especially if a dark background can be arranged. *Acer negundo* 'Elegantissimum' is similar but with bright yellow variegation.

Amelanchier canadensis presses hard to be considered the most beautiful small tree to find a home in our gardens.

It makes a tree perhaps twenty feet high and as much

through. It has two seasons of beauty; the first in April when its small pure white racemes of flower expand, while the leaves, then generally tinged with pink, are half grown and again in autumn when its leaves become rich red or perchance a dappling of red and yellow. No one who has seen it in these seasons is likely to fail to admire it or not wish to have it in their garden, though it must be confessed its season of beauty is fleeting. It needs nothing special in the way of soil so long as it is not over wet or very dry and it is perfectly hardy anywhere in these islands.

A native of North America, it was introduced by the 'tree-monger' Archibald, Duke of Argyll, in 1746. In its native land it has a rich variety of names, among them shad-bush, service-berry, grape-pear, and bloody-choak-berry. I prefer the commoner, though disputed common name, the snowy-mespilus. There is also a European snowy-mespilus, *A. ovalis*, which is a shrub and very beautiful too, but has less attractive autumn colouring.

Arbutus. The 'strawberry trees' are attractive, small, evergreen trees of 10–20 ft. They are exceptional in that, although in the Erica family, they will thrive on chalk and also on most other soils. The most commonly planted is *A. unedo*, the Killarney strawberry tree. It would be worth having in the garden if only for its unusual 'architectural' shape, its beautiful dark green leaves and above all for its dark red-brown trunk and stems, even if it did not flower and fruit. But of course it has both and most unusual they are. The flowers appear in autumn, even up to December, in drooping clusters, urn-shaped, and white. Slowly they change to green fruits which are round and roughly pitted. They bear no resemblance to a strawberry until the reddish orange flush of ripening appears next autumn. Thus fruits and flowers may be present together. These fruits are edible but I do not recommend them for flavour.

A hybrid between the above and the Grecian strawberry

tree (*A. andrachne*) is *A.* × *andrachnoides*. Here the winter bark is brilliant cinnamon-red and even more attractive than that of *A. unedo*. It seems quite hardy.

Birch. A tree which can stir a poet of Coleridge's stature to describe it as 'the most beautiful of forest trees' must have something special about it and indeed it has. Although there are some attractive birches from other lands, none is more beautiful at all seasons than our native *Betula pendula*. Its silvery trunk is an especial delight but is a very variable characteristic. It is one of those plants which are best seen before purchase or bought from a nurseryman with a reputation he would not care to lose. I like to see three planted close together so that they may grow together, usually at different paces, and make a most telling group or focal point. On sandy heaths, in upland bogs, high into the Scottish Highlands or on the chalky downs, in every one you may find the birch surviving when most other trees have looked for more promising territory. There are a number of very good clones, among the best 'Dalecarlica', the Swedish birch, a very elegant tree with cut leaves; 'Fastigiata', an erect form which makes a useful 20 ft screen, 'Youngii' just the opposite, a weeping birch.

Cercis siliquastrum. Called the Judas-tree, as some say its leaves are vaguely reminiscent of the fatal coins; others think that it was the tree upon which Judas hanged himself. Though grown in this country for more than three hundred years it is still not common. If you see a tree in May still leafless which looks as if it were emerging from a rosy-purple veil, it will be a Judas-tree. Come closer and you will find it bejewelled with rosy pea-shaped flowers set hard upon the trunk and branches wherever there is a joint. A remarkable sight. The light green leaves which follow are smooth and slightly glaucous. Plant while it is young as the thick roots are liable to rot off without replacement in an ageing plant.

Chamaecyparis lawsoniana. (Lawson's Cypress). This very good plant used to be found in catalogues under 'Cupressus'. They are now separated into those with flat branchlets and small cones (Chamaecyparis) and those having larger cones and rounded branchlets (Cupressus). More than 40 cultivars are now available, differing in foliage colour, size, shape, and habit of growth.

One of the very best is *C.l.* 'Columnaris'. It is especially suited to small gardens as it is slow-growing and rarely exceeds 25 ft, forming a dense column of glaucous blue foliage. Another is 'Ellwoodii', a charming, slow-growing cultivar having erect branches covered with delicate green-blue foliage. If you have plenty of room there is nothing better than 'Intertexta', very vigorous and distinct with its somewhat pendant habit. It has been called the most beautiful of all conifers. At the other end of the height scale is the 4-ft dwarf golden pyramidal 'Minima Aurea'.

If anyone has admired the very distinctive, tall, narrow Mediterranean cypresses but found they are too tender to grow here, they may well be glad to try 'Kilmacurragh'. It is a very beautiful bright green, extremely hardy and very similar in its effect on the garden scene to the Mediterranean cypress.

Cotoneaster. This large and distinguished family of berried plants contains at least one good small tree, *C. frigidus*. This will make a tree up to 25 ft high. Its white flowers are not especially distinguished but autumn sees the branches festooned with splendid clusters of bright red fruit. If spared by the birds they remain so until February. Seedlings are variable but mainly good.

Crataegus. The thorns are a large family. The pretty pink, red, and white spring flowering small trees are familiar to all; less well known but very good are:

C. × *lavallei*, a vigorous small tree producing numerous heads of white flowers each one inch in diameter in late spring, followed by large, orange-red fruits which may persist well into the winter. It is also distinguished by its long leaves, which often remain on the tree and green until December.

C. prunifolia, notable for its large persistent red fruits and polished dark green leaves, which colour magnificently in autumn.

Embothrium coccineum. The Chilean fire-bush is perhaps the most brilliantly flowered of all small trees – catherine-wheels of orange-vermilion clustered along the branches, shining with an ethereal brilliance, especially in the evening light; but a plant only for those with warm and sheltered gardens.

A fire-bush with narrower leaves is *E. lanceolatum*, considered by many to be even finer. This slender, graceful tree certainly is hardier and has survived 32°F of frost. It flowers in clusters along the branches as well as at the tips, so that the whole branch is clad in scarlet each May and June. It is an acid-loving plant admirable in rhododendron soils. It is a difficult plant to establish, needing a high rainfall and the shelter of other trees. About 1 ft is as large a plant as moves easily.

Fraxinus (Ash). The ashes have a flowering group, the *Ornus*. Of these *F. mariesii* is widely regarded as the most handsome, the flowers appearing in creamy clusters in June. Being of slow growth, it rarely exceeds 15 ft and is admirable for small gardens. The type-tree of this group, *F. ornus*, the manna ash, is a dense, handsome tree with luxuriant foliage. Decidedly ornamental in flower, its blossom has an odour some find disagreeable, so it is wise not to plant it near to the house. You can obtain manna sugar from the trunk by making an incision and collecting the sap which exudes from it.

Ginkgo biloba. The maidenhair-tree is a deciduous conifer and one of our most remarkable and distinguished trees. It forms an upright tree, bearing leaves of a most distinctive fan-shape, cleft about halfway and irregularly notched. It is thought to be the most ancient of existing flowering plants, the last representative of a race of trees which played an important part in the vegetation of an earlier stage in the world's history, as is well documented in fossil remains.

Gleditschia triacanthos. No tree in this family is worth planting for its flowers but this species is popular because of the beauty of its fern-like foliage and its attractive shape. It changes colour in the autumn to a spectacular, clear bright yellow. It is quite hardy and deserves more frequent planting. The cultivar 'Sunburst' is striking, having bright yellow, unfolding leaves. It bears formidable thorns, but the form 'Inermis' is thornless.

Gymnocladus dioicus. Kentucky Coffee Tree. A slow-growing and hence usually small tree which is rarely seen. A member of the pea family, producing greenish-white, unremarkable flowers, its glory lies in its foliage, which is pinnate, rather resembling that of an ash, but which may be as much as 3 ft long and 2 ft wide. It has been described as the most beautiful of all our hardy trees: the leaves are pink-tinted on opening, changing to grey-green, and then to a clear yellow in the autumn. Its common name is derived from the practice of the early settler in Kentucky and Tennessee of roasting and grinding the seeds to make a drink resembling coffee.

Ilex. The hollies have been cultivated in Britain for hundreds of years and have sported into almost as many cultivars. They are adaptable to all soils, make slow-growing, handsome, and enduring hedges, withstand clipping in April or September admirably, retain their dense growth to the ground and so make excellent shelter. Best transplanted in May, in common with most evergreens, provided it is not allowed to lack water. Out of the multitude of large-leaved, small-leaved, silver-variegated, gold-variegated, or otherwise remarkable cultivars the following can be highly recommended.

I. × *altaclarensis*, the broad-leaved or Highclere holly. Especially handsome, as are its clones 'Camelliaefolia', 'Golden King', and 'Hodginsii', the finest hedging variety, and 'Wilsonii', a female form which berries magnificently in favourable seasons.

I. aquifolium, the common English holly. There is no more useful evergreen. Excellent clones include 'Argenteo-marginata', 'Golden Queen', 'Handsworth New Silver', 'J. C. Van Thol', 'Madame Briot', golden edged and gold marked, and 'Pyramidalis', a non-prickly form, very free-berrying, in pyramidal shape and so making a good lawn specimen.

Laburnocytisus adamii. The purple laburnum. A plant for those who like the unusual, being a graft hybrid between laburnum and cytisus. It produces flowers of three types: some yellow, some purple, some a purplish-pink blend of the two in a process known as a chimaera, in which the tissues carrying the characteristics of the two genera twist and overlay so that a bud may produce any of the variables above. More a curiosity than a beauty.

Laburnum. This well-known, small, flowering tree, unique in its chains of golden flowers, needs no introduction. In choosing a species for the seaside there is much to be said for *L. alpinum*, the Scotch laburnum. It is particularly good for wind resistance and flowers a fortnight later than that other 'best buy' among laburnums, *L.* × *vossii*, which is earlier and has longer racemes of flowers.

Malus. These are the flowering crab-apples. With the ornamental cherries they contain some of the most spectacularly beautiful of all small trees, when in flower; when they are not, many of them lack grace. Some bear attractive fruits as an autumn bonus. My list (picked from 70 sorts) is short, as the crabs are not the best of plants for the seaside and can easily be overplanted.

Malus floribunda, the Japanese crab, escapes my strictures on form as it bears its remarkably-beautiful flowers, pale pink as they burst from their crimson buds, on gracefully-arching branches; 'Golden Hornet' has white flowers and is remarkable for the profusion of small yellow fruits which cling close to its branches well into the winter; 'John Downie' is the best fruiting crab and the bright, yellow-and-red, conical fruits regularly cause dissent in my garden between those who enjoy their beauty and those who covet the excellent crabapple jelly they make.

M. × *purpurea* and its near relatives *M.* × *eleyi* and *M.* × *lemoinei* are deservedly the most popular crabs. Symphonies in wine purple, they have deep crimson flowers, dark purplish green shoots and leaves. The fruits are light crimson-purple.

M. × *hillieri* is attractive and late flowering, the flowers being crimson in bud opening to a bright pink. A few crabs have attractive autumn colour, and a good choice for this feature is *M. tschonoskii*; it makes a pyramidal tree with white flowers tinged pink, but with its great glory its scarlet and gold autumn colour.

Nyssa sylvatica. The tupelo is a North American tree which has not been planted as often as its merits justify by those who can give it the moist, lime-free soil that it needs. It forms a handsome, glossy, oval-leaved, pyramidal tree which explodes into bonfire brilliance as autumn touches it off in scarlet and gold.

Oxydendrum arboreum. It seems strange that such an excellent plant, which has been grown in this country for over 200 years, should be so little planted, perhaps because it is very difficult to propagate and is usually raised from seed. As it is slow-growing, this makes the production

Handkerchief shows (*above*) the wind at full strength and (*below*) the tranquil zone created by the semi-permeable fence

A pear fruiting and flowering concurrently in autumn as a result of the freak storm of July 1956

Euonymus japonicus hedge in good condition in spite of full exposure

Red Hot Pokers (*Kniphofia*)

Senecio laxifolius

Yucca filamentosa

Acanthus mollis

Atriplex halimus

A tough but beautiful annual mallow, *Lavatera trimestris*

The white-collared sea-holly *Eryngium alpinum*

A pretty shrub for mild seaside gardens, *Hebe salicifolia*

The pampas-grass *Cortaderia argentea*

Above: a hedge of *Griselinia littoralis*

Right: The sea-buckthorn, *Hippophaë rhamnoides*, in fruit

Plants growing happily in the low pressure area on a wall in full exposure to the sea winds at Brighton

Holm Oak (*Quercus ilex*) sweeping right down to the beach at Goring-on-Sea

of the plant a long and laborious process and of course relatively expensive.

But, once established, what a tree for the autumn! It is one of the most brilliant that we possess. A few autumn trees like the Koelreuteria enchant us for a brief spell and then all too rapidly drop their glorious leaves to rot on the ground. *Oxydendrum* does not do this. Its leaves are very persistent and are not usually at their best until November. The colour is usually very deep red with more tints of crimson than of orange in it.

In this country the oxydendrum is rarely seen more than 20 ft, although if you seek it out in the woodland garden at Wisley it has a height of over 30 ft. It forms a slender, almost fastigiate tree, flowering only towards the top. The flowers are white and borne during July and August in lax panicles nearly a foot long. *Oxydendrum* is very welcome in that season, for there is generally no abundance of flowering shrubs in the woodland garden. But its real glory comes in the autumn and our gardens would be the richer if it were more freely planted.

Parrotia persica. This makes a 25–30 ft rounded tree which flowers about the end of February, but you have to look for them, for they are merely clusters of red-anthered stamens. Its great charm is its beautifully tinted foliage in autumn, mainly red with a hint of gold.

Paulownia. This is one of the great flowering trees. Imagine a pleasantly-rounded but sparsely-branched tree with largish, green foliage – a little too large for safety at the seaside – and in May, set upon the fresh green of spring, quantities of erect panicles of heliotrope or blue-purple flowers, as if the tree had suddenly become a bed of dark-blue foxgloves. Beware when planting that these blue flowers do not have to compete with the sky or the sea. Arrange a dark background or so that you may look down upon them.

They are not easy to grow or we would see many more of them. In their native China they do not have to contend with winters such as we have, for they produce their rather large flower buds in the autumn. After our stop-go winters it is small wonder that sometimes they fail to flower in the spring. They will grow almost anywhere, but flower only in the more climatically warm and consistent spots. There is a fine free-flowering group in the centre of Battersea Park in London.

Two species are to be recommended, *P. tomentosa*, the best known, and *P. fargesii*, more recently introduced, said to be better adapted to our climate, and flowering earlier.

Prunus. This enormous genus contains the plums, cherries, almonds, and peaches and among them there are a vast number of great garden beauty. I mention here only a few, which might be overlooked in a catalogue list running to approaching two hundred different plants.

P. incisa is generally grown as a bush but will make a small tree. It flowers before the leaves in March, every branch being covered with pink flowers – pink because the red calyx shines through the white petals. Most soils suit it. This cherry has a number of offspring, the best of which is *P.* 'Okame'. It forms a graceful, compact, hardy tree not too big for any garden, bearing a wealth of carmine-rose flowers in March.

Whatever else you miss, it should not be *P. subhirtella* 'Autumnalis Rosea', the glorious winter-flowering cherry. It is, when mature, a small and graceful tree perhaps 20 ft high and as much or more across. It is often worked on a 6 ft stem of mazzard (*P. avium*) stock which gives it height more quickly. Personally, I prefer it when started about 2 ft from the ground and then allowed to branch naturally. So treated, it makes a shrubby tree but, so delicate is the tracery of its branches and so light its tiny, rather birch-like leaves, that it provides the light shade so beloved of many semi-woodland plants quite ideally.

In mid-winter one could be forgiven for thinking that the first flurry of winter snow had fallen, for most of the tree's branches are dappled with clusters of small, white flowers springing forth from a warm pink bud. The cloud of blossom will last until well into the next month; then, until the first warm spell next spring brings forth another flush of flowers, we shall have to be content with the occasional cluster bursting into life, but I shall be most surprised if there is a single day when no flowers can be seen. Even through the snows of winter, this is true.

When choosing a place for this treasure, remember its beauty is not flamboyant, so a sheltered position near to passers-by, with a dark, evergreen background, has much to commend it.

It is also worth remembering that the fragrant flowers of the winter cherry will open well in water if budded shoots are cut and brought into a warm room, a pleasant habit that it shares with the almond, the peach, the flowering currant, and the forsythia. This pink form is superior to the normal white one.

The very fecundity with which Japanese Cherries produce their flowers causes them to bunch too closely to the branches. One that escapes this charge is *P. serrulata* 'Shimidsu Sakura'. It is late-flowering, in early May. It has large, many-petalled flowers about 5 in. across, perfectly white when fully out but pink in bud. These flowers are arranged in drooping clusters of three to six, with long stalks to the individual flowers as much as 4 to 6 in. long. This gives its flowering a grace which eludes many others. As it rarely exceeds fifteen feet it is a good small-garden plant.

This also applies to *P. yedoensis*, the best known cherry in Japan. A graceful early-flowering tree with almond-scented, blush-white, single flowers, it is one of the parents of that charming hybrid *P.* 'Pandora'. This, too, is a comfortable tree to have about, as its pronounced upright habit removes the need for a pruning saw, so that the generous number of one-inch, soft pink flowers can be enjoyed to the full.

Of the peaches which do not really enjoy our equable winters and lack of summer sun, *P. persica* 'Clara Mayer' seems to thrive as well as any. It is an exquisite tree in blossom, the flowers being double and shell pink.

The common almond is a universal favourite; you may consider a hybrid of it with the peach which is sold as *P.* 'Pollardii'. It differs from the almond in having larger, richer pink flowers.

Lastly *P.* × *hillieri* 'Spire'. It is often necessary to emphasize a vertical line in architecture. This plant, some 25 ft by 10 ft through, makes an attractive change to the conifers. The flowers are a soft pink and its autumn colours can be quite remarkable.

Pyrus. The pear. The name is often used for the plants which will be found under Malus in this book. The plant I would call to your particular attention is *P. salicifolia* 'Pendula', the weeping willow-leaved pear. Rather a clumsy common name for one of the most distinct and attractive shapes in the garden. In winter, its branches stream groundwards in a graceful flow, every inch the thoroughbred; in spring, leaves and flowers appear together and its full charm is revealed; the leaves a silken white and the flowers creamy white. It loses a little of its spectacular whiteness as the season progresses but is always an attractive grey. There is no more elegant tree to place at the end of a path or vista where it is desirable to attract the eye with a notable plant.

Quercus. Most oaks are large trees; so is the American species, *Quercus coccinea* 'Splendens', the scarlet oak, but it is slow growing and not likely to outgrow its station in the life of the planter, so it is included here. In summer, it is attractive with handsome, bright green leaves; in autumn, it is a star in the galaxy of brilliant autumn-colouring trees. It turns a glowing scarlet, which lasts even into December.

Sophora tetraptera. A most ornamental small tree from New Zealand. It is a plant for the warmer gardens, but so distinct and so elegant that it must not be missed by those fortunate enough to live in such parts. The foliage is pinnate, reminding one of fern fronds, delicately graceful; the flowers, in pendant clusters, are like no others but, perhaps the nearest comparison might be one of great golden fuchsias. In the form 'Grandiflora' they can be quite 2 in. long.

Sorbus. This genus includes the mountain ashes or rowans and the white beams. There are no more suitable trees for the medium or small garden, as they are economical as to space and have decorative foliage, and in the case of the rowans some of the most spectacular berries to be seen.

S. *aucuparia* is our native mountain ash and a variable species in nature but needs to take second place to none. Good cultivars are 'Asplenifolia', fern-like in foliage, and the yellow-fruited 'Xanthocarpa'.

S. *hupehensis* comes from China and has white fruits which turn a blush-pink as they age. Quite often they last right through the winter.

S. *intermedia*, the Swedish white beam, is among the most wind-resistant of trees. Forms selected in Sweden for wind hardihood are especially good. It makes a good hedge and bears bright red fruits when growing freely.

S. 'Joseph Rock' is a rowan with pale yellow fruits. If you have room for only one of this type and can bear the name, S. *pohuashanensis* could be your choice. Its clusters of berries are truly remarkable; they are orange-scarlet of intense brilliance.

Sorbus vilmorinii. There are few finer small trees than our native mountain ash, or rowan as the Scots would have it. This one is a Chinese relative which surely must run it very close. It is perfectly hardy and I know of no reasonably drained soil on which it does not flourish.

It has been said that this is the best shrub for all seasons to come out of China. High praise indeed, but consider its official description at the time of its Award of Garden Merit in 1953: 'It attains not too great a size, between 10–20 ft high, and is noted for its rather spreading habit and graceful arching branches. The dark-green, fernlike leaves, each pinnately divided into 19 to 29 leaflets and with attractive, red foot-stalks, accentuate the elegant grace of the plant. In spring, when the young flowering shoots appear, they are a delicate dull red, being covered with a rusty pubescence. Appearing in late May or early June, the white flowers are arranged in rather flat, loose clusters up to 3 in. across and are in no wise remarkable. But they set freely and each head of flowers is transformed into a handsome cluster of fruits which are attractive throughout the season until the end of October. At first they are a bright rosy red, but slowly the colour fades to pink and finally to creamy white with a faint flush. Delightful as this plant is at all seasons of the year, there is no doubt but that its main attraction lies in the changing beauty of its fruits.'

Surely there are few small trees to equal this?

Tilia. Most of the limes are large trees, but *T. mongolica* has much merit as a small tree of perhaps 30 ft; the lobing of the leaf is very distinct, giving an ivy-like effect.

Chapter 6

SHRUBS BESIDE THE SEA

INTRODUCTION – FIRST CHOICES FOR THE SEASIDE – OTHER GOOD SHRUBS

Possibly the most important plants in the garden are the shrubs. I imagine the questions an intending planter might ask himself are: 'What are the most beautiful shrubs which will grow in my garden? Where will they look most effective? Have they any special requirements as to soil, shelter, or pruning?' These I hope to answer in the succeeding list.

Introduction

Before looking at some of those plants which, for one reason or another, will tolerate these conditions, but are not seen in seaside gardens as often as their merit warrants, it must be emphasized that the most careful plant selection can be a waste of time if the rules for seaside planting are ignored. These are empiric and formed from common sense, but rarely found in a textbook.

Many people plant, as frequently advised, in late autumn before the soil temperature drops, but consider to what you are condemning your poor plants if you practise this beside the sea – probably six months of intermittent gales. Many an evergreen will die with such treatment before spring mainly from dessication. Such evergreen plantings are always best done in late April. This means using pot-grown plants if possible, and adequate measures to see they do not dry out.

The drill for planting has been described in Chapter 4, so I will not repeat it.

A very good case can be made for lavish planting by the sea. No single plant can hope to compete with the wind. It is, therefore, sound sense to plant closely in threes or fives or multiples thereof; they will quickly interlock and form one dense bush, proof against the worst the gales may do. Additionally, there is less upkeep as dense growth keeps down weeds.

Interest must be created by contrasting colours, such as grey with golden, purple, or dark green foliage, and by contrasting shapes, *eg*, fastigiate with rounded, horizontal branching with upright, etc. Thus for a rounded shape, there are the rhododendron and the choisya; or a horizontal, branching habit, *Viburnum tomentosum*; for an upright or fastigiate shape, the Irish Yew; for a pendulous or weeping one, *Genista aetnensis*; for slenderly and sparsely upright, *Spartium junceum*, etc. Remember to use contrasts sparingly. A single specimen or group of upright conifers in a bed of heathers can be most effective, but a frequent repetition is 'bitty' and irritating.

The same may be said of foliage colour. Purple, grey, red, etc, are admirable used sparingly. A golden elder contrasted with the red-purple *Rhus* 'Royal Purple' is a summer-long joy; the bright green *Acer japonicum* makes even more effective its near relative, the deep wine-red *Acer palmatum* 'Atropurpureum'; in winter what better contrast of bark than the bright red *Cornus alba* 'Westonbirt' with the yellow *Cornus flaviramea*? And so on. Such features, used sparingly, serve much the same purpose as statuary in a large garden. They give point and interest only because they are sparingly used and carefully placed.

First Choices for the Seaside

Any good nurseryman's catalogue will give you hundreds – perhaps thousands – to choose from. All have glowing descriptions and in the right place I am sure all are worth having. My purpose here is to select those widely acclaimed as the best of their kind with special reference to the seaside garden. Some have already been mentioned in Chapters 2 and 3. If a choice is something of an adventure in that its hardiness suits it better to the warmer coasts, this will be indicated.

Buddleia. The thirty years which have passed since I spent an ecstatic summer as a student at Wisley watching the wonders of the east in the shape of new plants opening before my eyes, have not dimmed the memory of my first sight of *Buddleia alternifolia.*

This particular plant had reached its full height of some 10 ft. It resembled a miniature weeping willow, with slender branches a yard long sweeping down towards the ground, set from end to end with tight bunches of blossom – a sheer waterfall of soft purple.

I decided then that it was a plant without which I could not garden. Alas, time has shown this to be impracticable. Since leaving Wisley I have always gardened on chalk and to my bitter disappointment its colour there is reduced to a dull and depressing puce-pink. However, for most there is no bar to this glorious shrub; it is quite hardy and, if it has a choice, prefers steep, dry banks, and open, warm places, where it grows like a fine leaved and very graceful weeping willow, a small tree, until its pendulous sprays erupt all along into tight bunches of soft purple blossom at the end of May – so generous that the whole shrub turns into a soft and weeping cascade of colour.

Nothing could be simpler than its cultivation. It needs pruning, so that many young shoots are made each year as, unlike other buddleias, it flowers on growths made in the previous year. Perhaps this is best done by pruning at least half the wood which has flowered, either hard back or to a strong young shoot immediately after flowering; this will induce the growth of those long, slender wands which the following May will burst into streaming cascades of colour.

B. alternifolia is best bought in a pot, as its roots tend to go straight down with little branching, making it somewhat temperamental at planting time. To increase it, half-ripened cuttings root easily in a cold frame and will make a popular gift to your friends.

Buddleia davidii is a much commoner shrub and a good seaside one; left unpruned it can make a useful windbreak. It is deciduous and takes kindly to severe pruning if one wants the splendid, 18-in. plumes it can produce on vigorous young wood from July to September. It has many good garden forms, among them 'Black Night', 'Empire Blue', 'Royal Red' (really deep purple) and 'White Profusion'.

Calluna vulgaris is the heather of Scotland and the ling of England and is too well known to need description, but it has shown a number of interesting variations, among the best being:

'Alportii' – crimson, tall, 2–3 ft, erect.
'Alba Plena' – dwarf, white, double, very free flowering.
'Barnett Anley'.
'County Wicklow' – dwarf, lilac-rose, double, spreading.
'Hammondii' – tall, white, attractive dark green foliage.
'H. E. Beale' – medium, pale pink, double, long flower spikes.
'Searlei' – medium, white, late-flowering.

The heathers are perhaps best grown in an open situation and a peaty soil. They will not grow satisfactorily on limy soils.

Camellias. The first plants of this very fashionable genus from the Far East seem to have been flowered at Thorndon Hall in Essex in 1739 but it was not until the end of the century that the tea clippers started to vie with each other in bringing home new varieties. The captains of these romantic sailers must have been keen or very well rewarded, for it can have been no easy job to keep plants alive for three or four months through storm and tempest and water shortages.

By the 1840s the camellia was at the height of its popularity as a warm greenhouse shrub – a quite unnecessary protection as it turns out. William Paul tells us that Loddige's Nurseries at Hackney were among the sights of London at flowering time. 'Many were thirty feet high . . . a perfect forest of camellias tenanted by blackbirds, thrushes, and other birds which build their nests in the trees . . . in splendid health and laden with blossoms.'

The varieties favoured were of what we would today regard as excessive formality and by the end of the century came the inevitable reaction and a decline in popularity. So the stage was set for the next phase of their development – their true role as a garden shrub. Who knows how the trend started? Perhaps someone's greenhouse fell to pieces and the astonished owner found his camellias flourishing as well if not better. We do know that one of the first outdoor plantings was made by G. F. Wilson in his garden at Wisley which he later passed on to the Royal Horticultural Society. Their success astonished many and the general effect was well expressed by a little girl who, walking round the garden at Wisley one spring day and seeing these camellias, exclaimed 'Look at the roses on the laurel bush!' At one time the camellia was called the Japanese-rose but no rose can match the beauty of foliage of a healthy camellia, deep green and lustrous. Some of these bushes are like this still. They have survived 36° of frost on more than one occasion. They are planted in light woodland where they rarely drop any of the flower buds that they produce so freely; these buds open successively, so that, even though frost in April and May brown some of the petals, there are others likely to escape. All these are forms of *C. japonica*, the first camellia to receive the Award of Garden Merit, in February 1930.

Another is *Camellia* × *Williamsii* 'J. C. Williams' which has been described as one of the best hybrid shrubs ever introduced to our gardens. Its parents are *C. japonica* and *C. saluenensis*. It seems to have all the virtues – amazing fecundity of flowers, complete hardiness and a very desirable habit of dropping its dead flowers which ensures it always looks well. *C. japonica* needs hard picking to achieve the same effect.

Another cultivar – possibly better – from the same cross is the first double-flowered child, raised by Colonel Stevenson Clarke at Borde Hill, and named *C.* 'Donation'. It is a delicious soft pink, some 5 in. across, not unlike a tiny double herbaceous paeony.

Two other excellent cultivars are the pure white *C.* 'Cornish Snow', a *C. cuspidata* × *C. saluenensis* hybrid, valuable for the freedom with which it produces its rather small, white flowers; and *C. japonica* 'Althaeflora'. This was raised as long ago as 1819 but is still one of the most desirable and free-flowering of carmine cultivars; its name means 'resembling a hollyhock', which indeed it does.

Carpentaria californica. A superb plant for maritime climates, but little planted. Given a mild site, a well-drained soil, it makes an attractive, bright green bush 6–8 ft high and as much through. It flowers in July in clusters of white, sweetly scented, 3-in. flowers not unlike

Japanese anemones. It can be raised from seed or by cuttings at midsummer, but these do not root readily.

Ceanothus. Shrubs with blue flowers are eagerly sought as there are very few. I doubt if there are better ones than the ceanothus, which can be grown out of doors in this country.

Ceanothus is available in either deciduous or evergreen forms. Of the former, the best known is *C.* 'Gloire de Versailles', which makes a rounded bush producing from July to the arrival of frost, large clusters of powder-blue flowers at the tip of its shoots. It is best pruned in April, thinning the shoots lightly; it can also be treated as an herbaceous subject cutting it to the ground annually. It will flower freely on the profusion of shoots so produced but should be liberally fed to sustain its vigour. An earlier bloomer of the same type is 'Indigo', an intensely deep purple from late May onwards. 'Henri Defosse' is a deep violet blue.

The evergreen species and cultivars are beautiful plants even when not in flower. Most have shining dark green, quite small, leaves borne on an arrangement of branches which is full of character. Among many good ones I like 'Delight', a splendid hybrid producing rich blue flowers in May and June on long panicles; it is one of the hardiest. *C. impressus* flowers about the same time but is quite distinct with its tiny leaves with deeply impressed veins and deep blue flowers. *C.* × *veitchianus* is a natural hybrid best given the protection of a wall; it flowers freely in June producing dense heads of bright blue flowers about 2 in. long. 'Autumnal Blue' is a first-class hybrid which makes a tall bush, with large, rich blue flower trusses in late summer and autumn.

Cistus. These are the rock-roses, exceptionally free-flowering about midsummer, fast growing, and evergreen. These are seaside plants par excellence. They enjoy full sun, hot, dry banks; many have aromatic foliage; many have gummy leaves which enable them to withstand salt-laden winds.

Of the latter, *C. palhinhae* is a little known and most worthy plant. It was discovered growing on sea-drenched rocks near Cape Trafalgar in Portugal. It is low growing, compact, with glossy sticky leaves and huge, 4-in., white flowers. 'Pat' is one of its offspring with 5-in. white-and-maroon flowers. 'Silver Pink' is one of the most beautiful natural hybrids; it grows to only about 18 in. high and has flowers of a soft, pleasant pink unusual in this genus.

C. × *cyprius* is hardy, vigorous, 6–8 ft high and bearing white flowers with five splashes of crimson around the yellow centre boss of stamens. Some of the best of the others are *C.* × *purpureus*, *C.* × *aguilari* 'Maculatus', *C.* × *skanbergii*, and *C. laurifolius*.

Cytisus. These are the brooms. A very large family much confused with Genista and recently with Sarothamnus. But there is no argument as to their beauty. They are especially well adapted to the seaside, for their elegantly slender growths bend and sway unharmed in the fiercest winds. Moreover the shoots of many are green and act as leaf surface should storm or spray temporarily put leaves out of action. They are very rapid growers, especially the clones of the common yellow broom; accordingly, if knifed back regularly, 'legginess' can be avoided. A poor soil seems a positive advantage; in such a place in full sun they will seed freely even among rocks and soon become as tough and unassailable as gorse. *Caution* – rabbits and hares are very fond of brooms. A little wire netting collar may be necessary.

Here is a small selection.

Cytisus albus, the Portuguese white broom, is a 10 ft plant of slender grace, best seen emerging in a shower of white bloom from other dwarfer shrubs.

Cytisus battandieri. This is one of the newest and the largest of the brooms, reaching 10–15 ft and flowering in June. It was discovered in Morocco in the Atlas mountains.

In foliage, it is perhaps the most remarkable of all brooms. The leaflets, borne in threes, are unusually large – some 2–3 in. long – and magnificent in a silvery down which glistens in the sun like shot silk, with a sheen which is dimpled and dappled as the breeze stirs the foliage. It grows vigorously and rapidly and seems to be hardy, in that it has survived 20° of frost in recent winters.

In June the tree is lit up with golden candles; each candle richly scented and made up of closely packed pea-flowers. Richly scented indeed – but of what? I always ask new visitors to my garden of what it reminds them. Nothing better has yet been said than: 'the scent of pineapple mixed with fruit salad.'

Once flowering well, you will probably have plenty of seed to give to your friends, but it is most difficult to strike from cuttings, even with the aid of footing hormones and mist propagation.

Cytisus × *beanii* is a charming, semi-prostrate hybrid bearing golden flowers, and *C. x kewensis*, disappears beneath myriads of creamy yellow pea-like flowers each April; both are fine shrubs to grow over a stony outcrop or low wall. *C. nigricans* is a very useful and elegant 3-ft, late-flowering shrub bearing yellow flowers continuously through the late summer. 'Porlock' is one of the most prolific plants of spring. Give it the shelter of a house recess if you can, so that you may enjoy the remarkable scent of its butter-yellow flowers.

C. scoparius (*Sarothamnus scoparius*), the common yellow broom or scotch broom. In its own right a fine plant for the difficult cliff top, but its real charm lies in the beautiful clones which have arisen from it: 'Cornish Cream', 'Firefly', 'Golden Sunlight', and 'Moonlight'.

Daboecia cantabrica. The Irish or Connemara heath. A dwarf, lime-hating plant whose main use is in the heath garden. The foliage is dark green and heath-like, terminating in 5-in. racemes from which hang the beautiful purple bells. There is a white form 'Alba', a dark purple 'Atropurpurea', and 'Bicolor', which has white and rose-purple flowers on the same plant.

Desfontainea spinosa. This magnificent shrub from the dark rain forests of coastal Chile is a late-summer evergreen, with foliage like a holly and striking scarlet and yellow tubular flowers. It grows if it likes you and is stubborn if it does not. Given a mild, moist climate, a rich, acid soil, and shade at the roots you should succeed. Superb on the west coast and occasionally elsewhere.

Elaeagnus. These are among the best wind resisters and have some most decorative coloured-leaf forms among them. *E.* × *ebbingei* is not nearly well enough known as a wind-resistant seaside shrub. It makes a handsome, tall, fast-growing plant with pointed, grey-green, glossy leaves; it will flourish at the base of thinning, taller trees and shrubs and so retain the shelter belt's efficiency. *E. macrophylla* is a beautiful, hardy, evergreen plant which will withstand both wind and full shade. Its large, firm leaves are silvered over when young and retain a metallic lustre beneath when fully grown, all the more effective for the soft, buff shoots upon which they are borne. It bears insignificant but sweetly-scented flowers in October-November.

Perhaps the most garden-worthy of all elaeagnuses is *E. pungens* 'Maculata', a slow-growing and very handsome golden-variegated shrub. It is worth a place in any garden.

Erica. This huge family, the main denizens of the heath garden, is so extensive that I list only the most outstanding:

E. australis 'Mr Robert', the white Spanish heath.

E. carnea. This, with *E. mediterranea* and *E.* × *darleysensis*, are the only species which will tolerate a limy soil. This they do very well and since they flower during the drab winter months, November–March, they are particularly desirable. They rarely reach 12 in. high. The most popular cultivars are: 'King George', 'Ruby Glow', 'Springwood Pink', 'Springwood White', and 'Vivelli'.

E. cinerea, the bell-heather. Flowers June–September. Good cultivars: 'C. D. Eason', 'Eden Valley', 'Knap Hill Pink', 'P. S. Patrick', and 'Rosea'.

E. × *darleyensis*, 18 in. November–March. Fine cultivars: 'Arthur Johnson', 'George Rendall', and the white 'Silberschmelze'.

E. vagans, the dwarf Cornish heath, bears its long sprays from July to October. Best cultivars: 'Lyonesse', 'Mrs D. F. Maxwell', and 'St Keverne'.

Erica arborea alpina. This is one of the tree heaths. There can be few men puffing at their briar pipes who know that the vehicle for their enjoyment is a piece of the root of a tree heather, not of wild rose. 'Briar' is a corruption of the French vernacular name for these gigantic heathers – *bruyère.*

Gigantic indeed they can be – up to 80 ft in the mountains of equatorial Africa – but in this country they rarely exceed 6 ft. Give them a position sheltered from the coldest winds and from early morning sun, which harms them after nights of hard frost. If damaged, their powers of recovery are remarkable; just cut them back hard in the spring and new growth from the base will restore them with surprising rapidity.

The form 'alpina' (which you must insist upon) produces a dense and sturdy bush, upright in habit and slow in growth. There are few evergreens whose green is so rich and bright in winter. I would be happy to plant it for this alone, but around March it cheers us on into spring with masses of ash-white panicles about a foot long, heavy with honey fragrance on a warm day.

Escallonia. The tougher members of this supreme seaside shrub have been dealt with in Chapter 3. Every one there mentioned is worth planting as a purely decorative shrub, but there are many others which appreciate a little shelter from the very worst of the winds. They flower from June until the autumn – an especially welcome time in the garden. Nearly all are in shades of pink and red, but *E.* × *iveyi* is a fine white, making an upright, splendidly glossy bush, 10 ft high, covered with large, pure white panicles in August and September.

The Slieve Donard Nursery, of Newcastle, Co. Down, Northern Ireland, has produced many lovely hybrids, the main characteristics of which are compact habit and graceful sprays of a multitude of smallish flowers. 'Apple Blossom' is a very attractive hybrid which bears pink and white flowers in July. Many hybrids have 'Donard' in their cultivar name; this is a reliable guide to a good cultivar. Some outstanding ones are 'Donard Seedling', a pink budded white; 'Donard Star', with very large rich rose-pink flowers and a 3 to 4 ft compact habit; 'Donard Radiance', deep pink and very compact; and 'Slieve Donard', apple-blossom pink.

All hybrids of recent years have failed to make the old *E.* × *langleyensis* a back number; its habit is more evergreen than some and it bears its bright rosy-carmine flowers on graceful arching branches. Another of exceptional value is *E.* × *edinensis*, a neat bush growing 4 to 6 ft and studded in July with bright rose-pink flowers.

E. rubra 'Pygmaea' can be recommended as a dwarf shrub for the rock garden; it bears crimson flowers.

Euonymus. For a change, here is a family which is probably better on chalk than other soils. A very variable family of both evergreens and deciduous plants. *E. alata* is a purely foliage shrub, signalized by the corky angles of its stems; but its main glory comes in the autumn, when its leaves turn a brilliant rosy scarlet.

E. europaea is our native spindle-tree, than which there is no more noble sight in the autumn when well laden with its rosy fruits which split open to reveal a cluster of orange-red seeds. It has a number of noteworthy children, among them the purple-leaved 'Atropurpurea', 'Fructu-luteo', and 'Fructu-albo', with yellow and white fruits respectively, and the most noteworthy, 'Red Cascade'.

E. fortunei (or *radicans*) is a creeping evergreen which could be used much more with advantage. It will creep over the ground, over rocks, or up the face of a wall for 20 ft or more. Bone hardy, there are several attractive coloured forms. 'Colorata' has reddish purple leaves; 'Roseo-marginatis' has a pinkish leaf border, and 'Silver Queen', has silver variegations.

The Japanese spindle-tree is described in Chapter 3.

Fuchsia. One of the indispensable plants beside the sea. Its name is so frequently mis-spelled that it may be worth reminding you that it was named after Carl Fuchs.

Whilst some species are usually seen as greenhouse plants, fuchsias generally are not nearly so tender as is sometimes thought – if the right kinds are chosen. It is doubtful if any seaside garden cannot grow them, if you accept that the more tender sorts may be cut to ground level in bad winters, but they shoot strongly from the base in spring. Hardy species include:

F. excorticata. This New Zealander makes a small tree in very favoured places like the Channel Isles. Its flowers are smallish violet and green and yellow and are followed by 1 in. black fruits. It produces bright blue pollen which has been used for centuries by Maori women as face powder. Much beloved by the birds who may become distinctly intoxicated, to the delight of cats who soon learn to wait for an easy victim.

F. magellanica. The variations of this South American constitute the most reliable of the outdoor fuchsias. *F. magellanica* 'Riccartonii', mentioned in Chapter 3, is the most widely grown. I have seen it happy in Yorkshire, in Edinburgh, and many places on the West Coast. Good tempered, with a very long flowering season, free flowering to the point of abandon, magnificently red and purple, easily propagated and wind tolerant.

Equally hardy, less spectacular, but more graceful is *F. magellanica* 'Gracilis'. It grew wonderfully well in the hills of my boyhood home in Cheshire with the help of a shovelful of dry weathered ashes placed around the collar and over the roots. Remove these ashes carefully when the danger of severe frost has gone.

F. exoniensis. Better known as *F. corallina*, it resembles *F. magellanica*, but has larger flowers and widely spreading branches. First rate against a white wall.

Hybrids. There are many readily-obtainable cultivars which may add more colour but perhaps less grace than the above. Examples are: 'Brilliant' (rose and purple), 'Display' (carmine and rose pink), 'Elsa' (violet-rose and white), 'Madame Cornelissen' (red and white, large flowered), 'Mrs Popple' (red and purple), and 'Tom Thumb', a very free-flowering, compact dwarf in rose and violet.

Genista. When the blooming of our native broom, the *Cytisus*, is over the exotic brooms take its place. The dwarf species are indispensable in the rock garden and the taller ones valuable summer shrubs. They need the same conditions as *Cytisus*.

Genista aetnensis, the Mount Etna broom, will grow to 12 ft or more and cascade its pendant green shoots almost to the ground, studded in July from end to end with tiny, golden pea-flowers.

G. cinerea has slim, silver-green, drooping branches

which bear a fragrant mass of golden yellow flowers in June. A very good early summer shrub.

G. hispanica, the 'Spanish gorse', is a must for any seaside garden. It is not unlike a dwarf, close-knit gorse. Planted on any hot, dry bank, it rolls out an undulating carpet of green mounds which, each May and June, turns bright yellow. Odd plants do tend to die out without reason. I have seen it thriving in apparently pure sand in full exposure with its toes in the sea.

G. lydia makes a two-foot pendulous bush, admirable among rocks or on a dry wall. Bright yellow in May.

G. pilosa is a native trailing shrub which is very useful for clothing banks. A sheet of gold for weeks on end in May.

G. tinctoria 'Flore Plena' is one of the best of all dwarf yellow-flowered shrubs. It is our native Dyer's Greenwood, from which the famous Kendal Green was made.

Griselinia littoralis. A somewhat tender New Zealand evergreen chiefly noteworthy for good habit and shining apple-green foliage. It is very wind-resistant. Excellent on the west coast and in such localities as the Solent.

Gorse (*Ulex europeus*). In Chapter 3 I have written about our splendid native plant with the enthusiasm that it deserves. It need not, of course, be used only as a hedge, but, if you use it in the pleasure garden remember its spiny nature.

Hebe. Perhaps still better known by its old names of veronica or shrubby speedwell. It is best to regard them as tender, for even the hardiest are likely to be killed in years when the frosts are severe. They are essentially seaside shrubs, withstanding sea spray better than most by reason of their ability to enclose their buds in leaves about to open, like hands in prayer. Generally speaking, the smaller the leaves the more hardy a hebe is. All are easily propagated by summer cuttings rooted in a frame. With the possibility of losing one's mature and treasured plants it is wise to have a few cuttings of each, rooted in frost-free frames, so that should the worst happen replacements can be readily made.

The species and cultivars can be roughly divided into those grown primarily for protection or for attractive foliage and those whose charm lies in their display of flowers.

FOLIAR HEBES

H. albicans. A dense, rounded grey-blue hummock, quite hardy. 2 ft.

H. anomala. Bright, shining green, compact, 4 ft. Useful in colder places.

H. brachysiphon (*traversii*). Free-flowering and nearly hardy. A good hedger.

H. cupressoides. Resembles a dwarf, grey-blue conifer, 18 in.

H. darwiniana. A most attractive species with narrow, spear-shaped leaves coloured blue-grey.

H. pinguifolia 'Pagei'. An excellent ground cover or rock garden plant, producing wide mats of glaucous grey. Always an attractive plant. Should be in every garden.

FLORAL HEBES

Quite the largest group arise from *H. speciosa* which I have introduced in Chapter 3. Among the cultivars are 'Autumn Glory', bright blue; 'Alicia Amherst' (royal purple), 'Gloriosa' (bright pink), 'La Séduisante' (crimson), 'Purple Queen', and 'Simon Delaux' (rich crimson).

Another group of hardier summer flowerers seem to have their origin in *H. salicifolia*, itself a good, rather tall, 7–8 ft plant. Among these the following are noteworthy – 'Hielan Lassie', blue-violet and, like all in this group, compact, narrow leaved, with long slender spikes of bloom; 'Midsummer Beauty', lavender; 'Spender's Seedling', fragrant white flowers. 'Great Orme' is one of the great cultivars, some 3 ft high, glowing from July to the frosts with bright pink, tapering spikes.

H. hulkeana. Freely described as the most beautiful of the hebes. I do not dissent – but it is difficult to grow and by no means hardy. Snug in a sheltered corner of the house, it can reach 6 ft and throw from the end of every young shoot lax panicles of pale lavender blue as much as 18 in. long. Keep a few cuttings rooted every year, for young plants flower best and are hardier.

Hydrangeas. One of the great seaside shrubs, in beauty over a longer period than any other.

Anyone can grow a hydrangea if he chooses the type suited to his own circumstances. Some flourish in the chequered sunlight of open woodland, some in full sun, and yet others beside the sea and nowhere else. But wherever you are there is an indispensable requirement for their health and happiness – proper soil preparation before planting. This means cultivating the soil deeply and digging in plenty of humus – decayed leaves, farmyard manure, and compost. You must then protect this reservoir from evaporation by a surface mulch of chopped bracken, half-decayed leaves, etc. All this is to satisfy the hydrangea's craving for water.

The ideal soil is a definitely acid loam; but hydrangeas will grow on chalk and on sands pretty well anywhere if you observe the cultural suggestions above. However, the soil has one very marked effect on the floral display. Hydrangeas are naturally blue, pink, red, white, or intermediates; all are influenced as to intensity of colour by the degree of acidity or alkalinity in the soil. It is idle, therefore, to pretend that the same cultivar – say 'Altona' – will be the same shade of pink in your garden as in mine unless our respective soils are of identical degrees of acidity. You cannot grow blue hydrangeas on alkaline soils without extensive, laborious, continuous feeding with iron and aluminium, which elements are prevented by alkalinity from absorption into the plant in its normal feeding process.

However, gardeners being what they are – very human beings – a challenge of this sort is quite certain to produce a determination to defeat nature in this respect. How can they best do it?

In my view – after gardening for over thirty years on chalk – the only way of producing blue hydrangeas in areas of high alkalinity is to choose the right varieties and grow them in containers, such as tubs, in specially imported soil with a pH of about 5. Anything else is expensive, most liable to failure and laborious. You are liable to be rewarded with muddied pinks and dull slaty blues rather than those glorious pure blues, purples, etc. White hydrangeas cannot be induced to blue.

THE pH ACIDITY SCALE. Do you understand the symbol pH? It is a scale to measure acidity, in soil among other things, which runs from 1 to 14, having neutrality at 7·0. The most acid soils likely to occur are about 3·5 and the most alkaline about 8·5. Acid soils therefore vary from 3·5 to 7·0 and alkaline from 7·0 to 8·5. From a hydrangea's point of view the best soil would be around 5·0 pH.

If you do tub, choose a naturally good blueing variety like 'Générale Vicomtesse de Vibraye'. When you tub up your plant in good 5 pH soil add about 1 oz of aluminium sulphate to the soil. When you water (with rainwater) in spring and summer, add ¼ oz of aluminium sulphate and ¼ oz of sulphate of iron to the water fortnightly; your reward should be gloriously blue.

IRON DEFICIENCY. A yellowing of the leaves, with stunted growth, is a familiar sight among hydrangeas on soils which are too limy. Usually it is due to a deficiency of iron in the plant. This can be cured by feeding with iron, which can be supplied by using Sequestrene Fe 138, obtainable at any good horticultural sundriesman. This is a specially available form of iron which, applied in solution, will quickly yield startling results. It has the demerit of being fairly costly and you may prefer to mix your own cure: sulphate of iron ¼ oz and sulphate of aluminium ¼ oz, dissolved in a little warm water and added to 2 gal. of water, applied to each suffering shrub. Start in spring, repeat fortnightly until the leaf colour returns and never, never let the plant become dry once you have started treating in this way.

PRUNING. It would be almost true to say that hydrangeas in the garden should never be pruned. They should not be pruned, for example, to keep them the right size, for you can choose cultivars which will fit any space from 12 in. to 8 ft both ways. Cutting back often produces non-frost-hardy young growth and the removal of old flower heads in the autumn is definitely detrimental, as the old heads are Nature's way of protecting the buds below during the winter.

In the spring you can remove dead wood, dead flower heads and thin weakly basal growth. If you are wise you will leave it at that.

PROPAGATION. No shrub is easier. A bottomless box half full of peat and sand and covered with a close-fitting glass lid in semi-shade will make an excellent propagator. For cuttings use half-ripe wood – *ie* just turning brown – from the end of a shoot from midsummer onwards. Cut off immediately below the second pair of leaves and insert firmly. They will soon root.

THE KINDS OF HYDRANGEA. For garden purposes three groups are readily discernible:

1. Wild species

Some of these are most beautiful.

H. aspera. Lance-shaped, softly hairy leaves. Large,

porcelain-blue flowers with lilac-pink bracts in June/July. For milder parts. 8 ft.

H. bretschneideri is more hardy. Tall, white, July-blooming.

H. villosa. It is doubtful if there is a more beautiful late-flowering shrub. An eight-foot bush covered in most of its parts with a down of hairs; flowers a clear blue even on chalk.

H. paniculata is a confident recommendation for the colder parts. The garden form 'Grandiflora' is the best. It produces massive cones of white, sterile florets. A most useful midsummer shrub.

H. petiolaris. A deciduous climber which will clothe a wall, even a north wall, or smother a tree, clinging like Ivy. White flowers freely produced.

2. Lace caps

An attractive name for an attractive group; the flower heads are flat, having a central area of small, unspectacular, fertile flowers surrounded by a fringe of showy sterile ones.

Some marked below are only suited to a shady, sheltered part of the seaside garden, but a must if you have these conditions. They make strong vigorous plants and are best unpruned. All are cultivars of *H. macrophylla*:

'Lanarth White'. Compact. Best for the small garden.
'Mariesii'.
'Whitewave'.
'Bluewave'. Best in shade.
× *H. serrata* 'Grayswood'. Best in shade.

3. Hortensias or Mop Heads

These, which are likewise cultivars or varieties of *H. macrophylla* need no description, as they are the hydrangeas familiar to all as a home decoration grown in a flower pot. By no means all such florists' cultivars are suited to the garden, however, still less to seaside gardens.

Anyone who has walked the cliff tops at Shanklin and other places in the Isle of Wight could be forgiven for feeling that mop-headed hydrangeas were easy and most desirable beside the sea. But all is not as it seems. The vast majority of these particular hydrangeas are the cultivar 'Joseph Banks', which I have mentioned in the chapter on hedges. Take it inland and the free-flowering habit disappears.

In breeding, its vigour, its massive stems, its huge flowers and its ability to grow in fullest exposure to sun and wind, particularly sea wind, have led to its use as a parent and the following of its children can be recommended. I give their colours in limy and acid soils respectively.

'Goliath'. Deep pink/purplish blue. Vigorous, tall, mid-season.

'La Marne'. Pale pink/blue. Huge heads. Tall, late.

'Madame de Vries'. Small edition of 'Joseph Banks'. Mid-season.

'Madame Legou'. Tall, white, late.

'Oriental'. Pink/mid-blue. Mid-season.

Should you not like or be able to obtain the above, it is probably best to rely on varieties of *H. macrophylla* normally grown inland, of which the following are some of the best:

'Altona'. Medium. Rose-red/deep blue. Mid-season.

'Ami Pasquier'. Dwarf. Crimson/wine-purple. Mid-season/late.

'Holstein'. Medium. Mid-season. Pink/sky blue.

'Madame E. Mouillière'. Tall. Mid-season. White. Won't blue.

'Mousseline'. Tall. Early. Pale pink/pale blue.

'Vulcain'. Dwarf. Mid-late. Crimson/purple.

'Westfalen'. Medium. Mid-season. Crimson/violet.

Hypericum. There are many shrubby St John's Worts, all of which are at home beside the sea.

H. olympicum is a gem to grow among the rocks of the alpine garden where its leafy stems can spread out. These are 4–5 in. long and bear grey-green leaves and pale golden flowers in clusters during July and August.

H. patulum in its form 'Hidcote' is perhaps the best of the hardy group. It grows to a height of 6 ft and as much through. It flowers continuously from June to September, bearing golden saucers of exquisite shape.

For the dry and shady place, a ground smotherer with great beauty in midsummer is *H. calycinum*, the Rose of Sharon. Each plant will rapidly cover a square foot and choke out any weeds.

Juniper. No one who has observed the juniper's resistance to the wind on the bleak downs around Salisbury or, bleaker still, in the Orkneys can doubt its hardihood. It is, moreover, a chalk-lover and seems to produce its carpet of blue-green wherever it is tried. A fine plant for the awkward bank. This is *Juniperus communis*. It has a number of cultivars which fit it for particular purposes. 'Aurea' is golden; 'Hibernica', the Irish Juniper, is a little column of grey-green admirable to give point in a formal layout, and 'Prostrata' explains itself.

J. horizontalis is a remarkable, bone-hardy, ground-hugging species. It makes a big plant 5 ft across and 2 ft high, grey-green in summer and steely blue in winter. *J. conferta* (*litoralis*) from Japan is another excellent sandy bank coverer. Within the garden one of the most 'architectural' shapes we have is *J.* × *media pfitzeriana*, dark green with pendant branch tips.

Kalmia latifolia. I would have to wrestle long before I was bold enough to write without qualification 'This is the most beautiful evergreen shrub I know', but I believe this is the plant I would choose. Camellias, rhododendrons, azaleas, and a multitude of others jostle for the title but without avail.

I think the mountain-laurel or calico-bush, its twin common names, earns its crown by the sculptured perfection of each part. Even before the flowers open each bud in the terminal cluster – which may have fifty or more flowers in it – has the fluted perfection of some parts in an exquisite watch mechanism; these open to a shallow bowl, each segment emblazoned and embedded with a brown anther; the whole a warm and friendly pink with deeper purple markings.

The leaves, too, add greatly to the attraction of the plant for they have a rich, glossy texture and a lively reflection. It flowers in May and June, following hard on the heels of the best of the rhododendron and azalea season.

The Kalmia will succeed in any slightly damp woodland or in a lightly shaded border, where it is perfectly hardy, but it must have an acid or neutral soil.

Leptospermum. The tea-trees or manukas of the Antipodes are seaside subjects restricted to the south-west and western coasts. They hate lime, need planting from pots and a good deal of sun to do well, when they may reach a height of 15 ft. The only species I have seen doing really well is *L. scoparium* 'Nicholsii' of which there is a larger-flowered selection 'Nicholsii grandiflorum'. The flowers, like multitudes of tiny potentillas, are rosy crimson.

Magnolia. These are not seaside plants save in warm, sheltered valleys, especially in the west. Elsewhere probably the best bet is *M.* × *soulangeana*, and its forms 'Alba Superba', 'Lennei', and 'Rubra'.

Magnolia stellata, however, has a special fitness for the small garden (though it grows very large at Dyffryn, in South Wales, and at Inverewe in western Scotland. It is an upright shrub which normally takes some years to reach even 5 ft; it has a bark which smells of lemon-scented verbena and starry white flowers quite freely produced at an early age. These have the strange sweet smell of broad bean flowers.

If these flowers were not so liable to weather damage it would be even more popular. However, if the first flush is damaged, a second but less abundant crop is produced. The flowers are produced before the leaves in March or April, white at first, then pinkish, having 12 to 18 petals, at first spreading then reflexed.

It will grow in any good soil containing leaf mould or other humus, preferably moist but well drained. It is one of the few magnolias which will give a reasonable show on chalky soils.

Medicago arborea. The moon-trefoil. A wind-hardy little plant with yellow pea-shaped flowers for the south and west coasts. It would be a better plant for the garden if it could make up its mind to flower all at once instead of frittering away its beauty over five months.

Myrtle (*Myrtus*). I would not like my garden to be without myrtle even if only for its legends. It was one of the favourite plants in early history, sacred to Venus, and to this day brides ask for a sprig for their wedding bouquets. Many have rooted these sprigs and have them in their gardens.

M. communis is the common species. I would plant the smaller-leaved, remarkably wind-resistant *M. communis* 'Tarentina'. Its fine leaf pattern, rounded, bushy shape and fragrant white flowers with a fuzz of stamens make it one of the best shrubs for planting against a house or near steps in a windy garden beside the sea. They are plants for acid soils in mild climates.

Olearia. The daisy-bushes or tree-daisies are a most extensive family and contain some of the most wind-hardy of all plants. These have already been described in Chapter 3. Very few are worth planting for their ornamental effect, but *O. semidentata*, is the best of all the flowering olearias; it is one of the finest of shrubs for mild maritime areas. Plant it in the open in full sun and it will reward you with a profusion of lilac, purple-hearted, daisy flowers each on a lax stem peeping out from slender silvery foliage.

Pernettya mucronata. It is doubtful if there is a better dwarf berrying evergreen; it hails from Magellan, at the tip of South America – not a place noted for its mild climate. It needs an acid, rhododendron type of soil and makes a stiff little bush about 3 ft high, clad with small, ovate, shining, evergreen, toothed leaves. From May to July it is covered with small, white, heath-like flowers. Its great beauty comes with its berries. These colour in the autumn. They are white, lilac-pink, scarlet, carmine, and blood-red. There they sit like lustrous, half-inch marbles through the winter to the following spring. They make good sprays for interior decoration. Pollination is better if a number of plants are set out in a group. 'Bell's Hybrids' and 'Davis's Hybrids' are both specially fine forms.

Phillyrea augustifolia is an excellent small evergreen maritime shrub. *P. latifolia ilicifolia* makes a small tree not unlike an olive and is happy on most soils. The best shrub in the family is *P. decora*; it has larger leaves, is dark green and bears many small white fragrant flowers in spring. These are followed by purple berries.

Phlomis fruticosa. The Jerusalem sage. This plant has evergreen grey-green leaves. The basal stems are woody; those made each year are soft and bear the large dense whorls of yellow stalkless flowers in the leaf axils at their tops in June. It is hardy in all but the worst winters and does not seem to mind what soil it is offered, but prefers a sunny bank.

Pieris. A species only for the sheltered wooded valley. If you have these conditions plus a peaty soil, *P. formosa* 'Forrestii' is superb. It is evergreen and makes a large bush which has its glory of flower in April, drooping panicles of fragrant white flowers like a giant but pendant bell heather. Quite as beautiful are the bright red young shoots. A particularly brilliant form has the name 'Forest Flame'.

Pittosporum. These are mainly evergreen shelter shrubs for mild seaside districts only. Most have very beautiful foliage, *P. tenuifolium* being grown freely in the South West to be cut for florists. It is a charming shrub with pale green leaves, lightly ruffled like the edge of a pie-crust, and black twigs. I think it is probably hardier than sometimes thought and worthy a try if in doubt.

The hardiest is *P. ralphii*, which has stood 20°F of frost. *P. tobira* can be planted for its flowers. It has bright, glossy, rhododendron-like foliage set in whorls and delightful clusters of orange-scented, cream flowers. Visitors to Monaco in spring will have seen much of it, which will lead you to think it is only for the very mild spots; against this you can set the fact there are excellent plants in the open in Battersea Park in London.

Rhododendron. This enormous family, which ranges from tiny prostrate alpines to those with enormous leaves, like a Zulu shield, is not a good choice for the seaside garden. The chances of success are so slender that no recommendations are made.

Rosemary. A seaside shrub par excellence. It is in fact a very much better plant where it can smell the sea than inland. *Rosmarinus officinalis* is the common rosemary which will make a dense bush up to 6 ft high and as much through; its aromatic foliage is always a pleasure increased by its pale blue flowers in May. There is an upright form, 'Pyramidalis', which is a boon to the small garden, and two better blue-flowered forms in 'Severn Seas' and 'Tuscan Blue'.

Quite distinct, with grey-green needles rather than leaves, giving the plant to my eye a rather fussy appearance, and bright blue flowers, growing compactly to 4 ft, is 'Benenden Blue'.

Roses do not come within my brief and it is sufficient to say that all can be grown in any seaside garden given the direct shelter recommended for all.[1] But it may be noted that the Scotch or Burnt rose (*Rosa spinosissima*) grows naturally in sandy dunes by the sea and spreads freely; there are several good cultivars. The beautiful rugosa rose also enjoys a sandy diet, but not a chalky one.

Rubus. These are the brambles; not a word to evoke much enthusiasm except perhaps as bramble jelly. Our hero in this note, however, a visitor from the New World, is one who has not had as many garden doors open to him as his excellence deserves. This is *Rubus deliciosus*. Few people in this country would agree that its fruit is entitled to the epithet 'delicious', but it is worth a place in any garden for its tremendous show of flowers.

It is a deciduous bush about 6 ft in height; its branches are thornless and, when young, covered with a white down. The flowers are pure white about 2 in. in diameter and borne in great freedom on short side branches from the previous year's growth during July and August. It thrives best in an open sunny spot, is bone hardy and not particular as to soil. Pruning can be confined to the occasional removal of the oldest canes.

One hundred and thirty years after *R. deliciosus* was introduced, Captain Collingwood Ingram crossed it with *R. trilobus*. The outstanding child of this happy marriage was *R. tridel* 'Benenden'. It is a vigorous shrub perhaps 12 ft high; each May its arching branches are bejewelled with an exuberant abundance of single white flowers. It seems to have inherited the best qualities of each parent – from *R. trilobus* a better habit, from *R. deliciosus* flowers of

[1]See *Roses for Small Gardens*, by C. E. Lucas Phillips, in this series.

greater substance and freedom and more attractive foliage. It is easily propagated by layers or cuttings.

Santolina. The popular and easy lavender-cotton. A singularly inappropriate name, for it seems to have no connexion with either plant. It is fated to wrestle with difficult names, for it is properly *Santolina chamaecyparissus* in its most popular form. It is of particular use and charm as a low-growing plant at the front of the border and is perhaps the whitest of all hardy shrubs. It is rarely more than 18 in. high and is reinforced by yellow, hemispherical flower-heads which are attractive if freely produced; otherwise they are best clipped away so that you may enjoy the frosty grey. This colour is encouraged if the bushes are clipped over in spring to within an inch or two of the ground. The leaves are aromatic when rubbed lightly. An even dwarfer form is *S. chamaecyparissus* 'Nana'.

S. virens is somewhat similar but bright green.

Senecio. A maritime family from New Zealand which contains some of the toughest plants we know, but very few have real pretentions to beauty. The only species I would plant is the fine *S. laxifolius*, which I have described in Chapter 3. It may be used anywhere in the garden, whether as a single shrub or as a hedge.

Spartium junceum. Here is a plant for a windy spot near the sea and one which has been grown in this country since the first Elizabeth. Any plant capable of surviving a 400-year test must be something special.

We give it the common name of Spanish broom although it seems doubtful if the Elizabethans allowed it such a then hated epithet. Naturally, it grows in regions of very restricted moisture; as a result it has almost entirely dispensed with leaves and relies on round, green, rush-like stems to do their function. This gives it the valuable attributes of wind tolerance and resistance to salt spray.

Its general shape is similar to our native broom but it

will grow to about 10 ft in height and is apt to be 'leggy' unless hard pruned when young. I find it best to plant an even number some 4 ft apart and to prune every other plant to the ground each year; thus the bright yellow, fragrant, pea-shaped flowers are borne in terminal racemes 12 to 18 in. long from June to September on alternate plants. This is quite sufficient to clothe the area and at the same time prevents the shrubs ever becoming too big for the small garden.

Seed, freely produced, is the best method of propagation. Young plants should always be bought in pots, as they resent root disturbance. It is quite hardy and will grow in any soil although light ones suit it best.

Tamarisk. Speak to most people of tamarisk (or tamarix) and I think the picture which rises to their minds is of a somewhat gaunt seaside hedge. These are usually the extra-tough sorts I have recommended for the 'Outer Zone' in Chapter 2. There are at least two other species worthy of a place in any garden for their more positive beauty.

They are the spring-flowering *T. tetandra* which flowers on the previous season's shoots and must, therefore, be pruned immediately after flowering, and *T. pentandra* (*hispida aestivalis*) which flowers in August on shoots made the same year, making winter pruning permissible without fear of cutting out flowering wood. So pruned, the shrub is a mass of light, feathery branches which at high summer are tipped with exquisite pink plumes a foot long.

Tamarix parviflora is familiar to those lucky enough to be able to seek the sun around the Mediterranean in spring. It bears its pale pink flowers on slender arching branches with whose deep vinous purple they make a happy contrast. Prune away the old spent wood after flowering.

Propagation could not be easier. Any pieces from the size of a small walking-stick downwards may be pushed into cultivated ground to about 12 in. depth in the autumn and will root in a single winter.

Viburnum. This very large family has few representatives that are good seaside shrubs. *V. tinus* is a noteworthy exception. There are so many viburnums spectacularly beautiful in flower and berry that this old and trusted friend, the laurustinus, could easily be overlooked. It is in fact one of the toughest of all the evergreens, not fastidious as to soil or situation; very hardy and wind-resistant. It will attain a height of 8 ft and flowers during the winter. It has a larger leaved, tougher form 'Hirtum', which is specially valuable at the seaside, where its suspect hardiness is called to less account. 'Eve Price' has a most attractive habit of producing pink flowers from clusters of carmine buds. It can be strongly recommended rather than the type.

Our native guelder-rose, *V. opulus*, is also notably tolerant, if given the close relationship with other plants that hedgerow ancestry demands. Other viburnums, as grown inland, include many of great floral beauty, which, in the main, require careful choice of site in seaside gardens.

Yucca. These are seaside plants par excellence. They revel in the warmer summers and will cheerfully put up with the hot dry bank. The leaves form a rosette of dark green Roman swords from the centre of which rises a towering spire of creamy-white pendant tulip-shaped cups. There are over a dozen species to try but the best bet is *Y. filamentosa*. This will flower annually, producing spikes up to 6 ft high. For spectacular foliage effect and rarer flowering *Y. gloriosa* 'Nobilis' (Adam's Needle) is an excellent plant.

Other Good Shrubs

In addition to the foregoing, the following shrubs do well

at the seaside as well as inland, if the situation is not too exposed. For details, see catalogues of the best nurserymen or good specialist books.

Abelia × grandiflora. Elegant semi-evergreen. 5 ft. White sprays.

Aesculus parviflora. Dwarf horse-chestnut. 8 ft. Spreading.

Berberis. I have mentioned the best of the evergreen barberies in the chapter on hedges. There are also many fine deciduous species and hybrids, such as the coral-berried *B.* × *rubrostilla* and the copper-leaved *B. thunbergii* 'Atropurpurea', together with several attractive dwarfs, evergreen, and deciduous, nice for low hedges or the larger rock garden.

Caryopteris clandonensis. Charming blue flowers in August/September. In late winter cut back the old flowered stems to a few inches from their points of origin.

Chaenomeles, the Japanese quince. For walls or open ground.

Chimonanthus praecox (or *C. fragrans*). The winter-sweet, priceless for the heavenly scent of its small flowers in winter. Rather slow.

Coronilla glauca. Scented, yellow pea-flowers. For warmer coasts.

Cotinus coggyria. Better known as *Rhus cotinus*, the smoke-bush.

Cotoneaster. A magnificent family of a wide range.

Deutzia. Easy shrubs in white or pink.

Enkianthus campanulatus. For lime-free soil in semi-shade.

Forsythia × *intermedia*. 'Spectabilis' and 'Lynwood'.

Fothergilla major. For rich autumn colour.

Garrya elliptica. For its winter catkins (male form).

Halimiocistus sahucii. Ground-hugging. Very hardy.

Hamamelis mollis. Witch-hazel. Glorious in winter.

Hibiscus syriacus. The best variety now is 'Blue Bird'.

Hoheria lyallii. For warm places. Pendant white flowers.

Honeysuckle (*Lonicera*). Scented and unscented in wide variety.

Jasmine. *Jasminum officinale* is the old white jasmine, celebrated for its scent. *J. nudiflorum* is the popular yellow one commonly grown on walls. For warm climates there are several other splendours.

Kerria japonica. An Everyman's shrub.

Leonitis leonurus. The 'lion's tail'. Tawny-orange flowers in September. For mild districts.

Lespedeza thunbergii. Rosy-purple clover flowers. Easy.

Leycesteria formosa. 'Elisha's-tears', 'Grandmother's-curls', etc. Drooping clusters of purplish flowers.

Mahonia. Grand evergreen shrubs for winter especially. Go to a top nursery and order *M. japonica*.

Osmanthus delavayi. Top-ranking evergreen scented shrub.

Osmarea × *burkwoodii*. Child of the above. Larger.

Philadelphus. Often mis-called 'Syringa'. White flowers, often scented. Tall and dwarf varieties.

Potentilla fruticosa. Flowers the whole summer, usually yellow.

Pyracantha. Fine berrying shrubs for walls or the open.

Ribes sanguineum. Flowering currant. Easy.

Romneya coulteri. The 'Californian tree poppy'.

Rue. *Ruta graveolens*. 'Jackman's Blue' is the best.

Skimmia japonica. Dwarf evergreen. Tolerates wind and shade. Some are unisexual and need males and females.

Solanum crispum. Scrambling climber for a warm wall.

Stranvaesia davidiana var. *undulata*. Fine red-berried evergreen.

Syringa (lilac). In great variety. See also Chapter 3.

Weigela. Useful and fairly wind-resistant. Several varieties.

Chapter 7

PARTICULAR PROBLEMS

BORDER PERENNIALS – BULBS – ANNUALS – LAWNS – FRUIT – VEGETABLES

The plants we shall discuss here are mainly, but not exclusively, the herbaceous perennials – those with annual stems which die away in the autumn leaving their hardy roots safely tucked away beneath the soil for the winter. They form an important way of adding summer colour to the garden with a minimum of labour. Inland gardens can have eight months in which some perennials are in flower, but beside the sea we are restricted to choosing plants which are naturally short, to obviate the danger of their being flattened by the first gale.

So out go the lupins whose hollow stems will snap or bend before the merest breeze; out go the delphiniums which must be staked; out go the taller michaelmas daisies for the same reason, and also for their rank untidiness unless skilfully tended; out, too, for their short lives go the aquilegias, geums, etc. Rather let us look for plants which are tough enough to smile as they bow to the wind; which are not over aggressive for space; which flower for a long period or have great beauty of shape; and which are likely to flourish without excessive attention.

I would suggest that the herbaceous borders of our parents and grandparents are no place to grow our perennials today. Much better that they form part of the mixed border which will form the inner face of many an exposed garden, or better still that an island bed surrounded by lawn be formed, shaped perhaps like a kidney and in which a succession of these attractive plants may find their home. Thus they can be viewed from all sides and, having all-round access to light and air, form sturdier, generally more healthy growths. If I say they require a well-drained, well-dug, well-manured soil, this is the ideal soil, but you should try to get as near as your circumstances will allow.

You have been advised to plant closely in other places in this book; nowhere is it more necessary than among the hardy perennials. About five plants per square yard is a rough and ready rule, with three or four plants of one kind in each group. It works out at about 12 in. between plants and 18 in. between groups. Since we are to keep our selection of height down to 3–3½ ft, 6–8 ft is as wide as your island bed can be to retain due proportion.

Planting is best undertaken from mid-September to the end of October, but in the warmer, drier regions which embrace most seaside gardens, any open weather up to the end of March is suitable. Plant firmly about an inch deeper than the plant was in its nursery. Soak in well.

Subsequently maintenance is mainly keeping the ground hoed clean of weeds; staking with brushwood (see annuals) if you have any floppy plants; thinning the shoots thrown up from the base when well established. Phlox and similar subjects benefit if half the shoots produced are removed right back to the root. Try to do this when the shoots are about 6 in. high. Most subjects will need lifting, dividing and the youngest bits replaced every, say, five years. Do not try to dig through the bed in winter; you may do great damage to the roots. Pricking over with a fork to a depth of 2 to 3 in., so that weeds can be removed or buried, is all that is necessary.

Although the list of plants included in this chapter contains thoroughly reliable seaside perennials and the best cultivars of those species so far as I know them, inevitably there are a few plants which have particular qualities which fit them especially for the seaside garden. Such a plant is the New Zealand Flax, *Phormium tenax*. A striking plant, indeed, which makes a dramatic clump planted in a group upon the lawn. It is not unlike a giant 6-ft stiff grass with sword-shaped leaves throwing spikes of slim lily-like buff flowers at midsummer. A row will make an excellent filter hedge, capable of standing up to the fiercest gale even if planted right in the sand. Another grass which is well known is the pampas-grass, *Cortaderia argentea*. This can form a similar statuesque lawn plant and seems impervious to the gales, its famous plumes being thrown up after midsummer when high winds are least likely.

The bear's-breeches, *Acanthus spinosus*, requires rather more shelter, but is another plant of 'architectural' shape. None more so, for its distinctive, spiny, toothed leaves were a favourite motif on Greek friezes on both their temples and vases. Towering out of these leaves come their 4-ft spires of flowers, each with 60 to 70 purplish white flowers, protected by a hooded bract with a single sharp spine. Most distinctive and long lasting.

Less statuesque but with an outstanding role as a contrasting shape among other plants are the sea-hollies. They are striking plants with teazle-like, steely-blue flowers. They have deeply rooting, fleshy roots which were, long ago, happy enough growing wild on sandy shores. This echo of their past makes them outstanding plants for coastal gardens, especially July to September, when most of them flower. *Eryngium alpinum* is the shortest, about 2 ft. The flowers are large and silvery blue; even the upper stems are suffused with blue. 'Violetta' is a larger edition with large violet blue flowers and upper stems. *E.*

tripartitum is an excellent plant, tall – 3½ ft – for a seaside herbaceous plant, but it carries very many, small, light-blue heads on widely branching stems from July to September. They can easily be propagated by root cuttings.

The globe-thistles, the *Echinops*, are good seaside plants but really too tall. They have long, grey-green leaves with fierce spines and flower as globular, blue spheres on straight stiff stems in July and August.

Quite the most spectacular vegetable is the globe-artichoke, *Cynara scolymus*, but it can have a place in the flower garden as a matter of right, for not only are its massive, deeply cut, and indented grey leaves as spectacular as any plant possesses but also its flowers, like giant blue thistles, are highly decorative. They, of course, provide the vegetable delicacy by their swollen bracts.

Another plant direct from the seashore is the sea-kale, *Crambe cordifolia*. It does not care how near the sea it finds itself. It will root deep even into shingle and from this thongy root comes broad thick greyish, cabbagy leaves; in June comes a foam of white flowers. To cover a shingly bank in full exposure, *C. maritima*, the common, wild sea-kale, has few superiors in its powers of pure survival.

With a name like sea-lavender it is difficult to imagine any home for *Limonium latifolium* other than a coastal garden. They are long lived, easy, hardy plants given sun and good drainage. This is a first-rate perennial for any garden which has space for a plant covering a square yard with delicate-looking but tough sprays of tiny flowers which can vary from light mauve to a quite deep lavender blue. Good cultivars include 'Blue Cloud', light blue, 'Chilwell Beauty', deep blue, and 'Violetta', violet blue.

In a crevice in the cliff face at Brighton, a few yards from the sea, there thrives a huge plant of *Cineraria maritima*, or more properly, *Senecio cineraria*. I have seen only stocks, red-hot-pokers, and occasionally wallflowers among the herbaceous subjects in similar places. This is a delightful silvery foliage plant with fern-like leaves. For bedding purposes there is a specially fine near-white variety, 'White Diamond'.

Lastly, the *Kniphofias* or red-hot-pokers. I can hardly think anyone who has not seen them luxuriating on the north-east coast at Whitley Bay – not our most hospitable coast – would realize what a first-rate seaside plant this is. They are a strangely neglected race especially by seaside gardeners for whom they are one of the very best herbaceous plants.

Ask anyone to find you a plant which will resist the stiffest wind, tolerate salt spray, have self-supporting flower spikes, achieve noble proportions as individual specimens, need little attention, flower – by selecting varieties – from June to September and above all have real character, and he will be hard put to find another to beat the red-hot-pokers.

Culturally they detest bad drainage; naturally they do well on warm, sandy soil but they come to no harm in colder, damper climes if the leaves are bunched together in early winter to prevent undue moisture and snow from settling in the corners where it could freeze. This can be untied in spring when it will fall back into its natural graceful form.

Try to see, by watering or mulching, that they do not dry out when coming into flower. It makes all the difference to those fine tall spikes.

You can increase their numbers by division but do not start until the new growth commences in the spring and make sure that the cut up pieces do not dry out in the critical weeks immediately after planting.

If I could only recommend one variety I think I would choose the fool-proof 'Royal Standard' with its 3-ft spears of scarlet and gold at midsummer. But I would hate to leave out 'Maid of Orleans', whose spikes of ivory-blush last so long.

For those who like species a little out of the ordinary, *K. galpinii* is a charming late flowerer, not more than 2 ft high with most attractive, slender, rush-like leaves from which spring spires of deep orange flame. Not a plant perhaps for gardeners in a very exposed spot; they may be better with *K. uvaria nobilis* – 6 ft of scarlet and gold magnificence!

Other worthy and usually available varieties are 'Bees Flame' (3½ ft), 'Bees Lemon' (3 ft), 'Gold Else' (3 ft), very free-flowering and long-lasting; and the late 'Lord Roberts' (3 ft) a deep tangerine orange and most free-flowering.

OTHER PERENNIALS FOR THE SEASIDE

Achillea 'Moonshine' and *A. taygetea*
Aconitum 'Bressingham Spire'
Agapanthus africanus 'Mooreanus' and Headbourne Hybrids
Ajuga reptans 'Multicolor'
Allium cernuum
Anemone × *hybrida* 'Alba', 'Bressingham Glow', 'Max Vogel', and 'Queen Charlotte'
Anthemis sancta-johannis
Armeria maritima 'Bloodstone' and 'Vindictive'
Aster acris nana
Aster amellus 'Advance', 'Bessie Chapman', 'Mauve Beauty', and 'Sonia'
Bergenia cordifolia and *B.* 'Ballawley'
Campanula glomerata dahurica
Centaurea dealbata 'John Coutts'
Coreopsis verticillata
Dianthus 'Doris'
Echinops ritro

Erigeron 'Darkest of All' and 'Dignity'
Euphorbia griffithii and *E. polychroma*
Geranium armenum and *G. sanguineum* var. *lancastriense*
Gypsophila 'Bristol Fairy'
Helenium 'Moerheim Beauty' and 'Wyndley'
Heliopsis 'Golden Plume'
Heucherella 'Bridget Bloom'
Iris germanica
Lavatera trimestris
Lychnis viscaria 'Splendens Plena'
Lythrum virgatum 'Rose Queen'
Nepteta × *faassenii*
Oenothera fruticosa 'Yellow River':
Penstemon 'Garnet'
Phygelius capensis
Physostegia virginiana 'Vivid'
Polygonum affine 'Darjeeling Red' and *P bistorta superba*
Rudbeckia speciosa 'Goldsturm'
Salvia × *superba* 'East Friesland'
Sedum 'Autumn Joy' and *S spectabile* 'Brilliant'
Solidago 'Golden Mosa'
Stachys lanata 'Silver Carpet'
Venidio-arctotis grandis
Veronica longifolia subsessilis 'Hendersonii'
Verbascum 'Cotswold Beauty'

Bulbs

Under this title I include all those plants which have adapted themselves to a form of underground food storage – bulbs, corms, tubers, rhizomes, etc, which require the same sort of treatment. They form one of the most rewarding kinds of plants that can be grown in windswept, seaside gardens. The underground food storage arrangements mentioned above mean that they have a secure base unaffected by tempest; further, the generally higher temperatures and sunshine provide the ripening conditions beloved by bulbs.

Bulbs are the joy of the impatient gardeners, since you buy an embryo flower already built into its structure; you only have to give it the conditions in which it can produce a good root system for the flower to appear. In the garden this means any well-drained fertile soil; usually the warmer and drier the better.

The choice of species is determined by the place in which you wish to grow the bulbs. In flower beds, for example, the hybrid tulips, hyacinths, daffodils in spring and gladioli or tuberous begonias in summer are particularly suitable.

They really come into their own in the rock garden, especially the dwarfer kinds whose stature is in proportion to their surroundings. They will associate with ease and charm with so many alpines, giving pockets a double season of interest. It is a mistake, however, to believe that you can plant them through a thick carpet of, say, aubrieta. They will flower the first year, but rarely do they get sufficient ripening of the bulb to allow them to increase and multiply happily. Plant in little groups where their foliage can grow freely and the bulbs obtain the hot summer sun which most of them love.

The fact is that pretty well the whole twelve months can be spanned by bulbs if thought is given to the choice of species. The crocuses are a good example. The earliest start to flower in late August. *C. speciosus* starts then and may go on to October. It is easy to grow with flowers varying with variety from deep blue to lavender and white. 'Oxonian' is a very good blue. At about the same season is *C. zonatus*, a robust rosy lilac; *C. niveus* is a November white. In December you can have the deep mauve-lilac *C. laevigatus*; in close succession in January and February will come *C.*

imperati, lilac-mauve, *C. tomasinianus*, a freely-spreading lavender-mauve, the yellow *C. susianus* and *C. aureus*. Soon come the numerous family of *C. chrysanthus*, surely among the most beautiful of all crocuses. Special favourites are 'Blue Bird', purple-blue overlying white, 'Cream Beauty', 'E. A. Bowles', deep yellow, 'Snow Bunting', and 'Zwanenburg', a symphony in orange, bronze, and mahogany.

So we come to spring with a host of other notable crocus species such as *C. minimus*, *C. sieberi*, and *C. versicolor*, and the very much more familiar, large-flowered, garden varieties, often call Dutch varieties, most of which have been derived from *C. vernus*. Good varieties include 'Joan of Arc' (white), 'Vanguard' (lilac), 'The Bishop' (purple), 'Nigger Boy' (maroon), 'Dutch Yellow', and 'Striped Beauty'. This type can be planted as late as November. The early-flowering species are best put in as soon as you can get the bulbs, usually July or August.

An even wider band of the seasons, mid-August to mid-May, is covered by the delightful dwarf cyclamen. First come *Cyclamen europaeum* and *C. neapolitanum* with its exquisitely marbled foliage, then *C. cilicicum* and hard on its heels comes *C. orbiculatum*, with its multitude of varieties and hybrids, and then *C. repandum*.

The smaller species of narcissus are well suited to the rock garden, especially if they can be used in pockets which are near to eye level, so that their delicate grace can be truly appreciated. *N. asturiensis* is a perfect miniature of a large trumpet daffodil some 3 in. high. *N. minor* is a little larger. Quite delightful is the angel's-tears, *N. triandrus* 'Albus'; about a foot high, it may have three or four flowers to each stem, occasionally six pendulous creamy bells.

Do not miss those delightful miniatures of the Dutch Iris sold at the florists. These are the cultivars of *Iris reticulata*. I like the pale blue 'Cantab' and the deep red-purple 'Hercules'.

There will be little need to remind readers of the charms of snowdrops, of the grape hyacinths or *Muscari*, of the scillas or of *Chionodoxa*, the glory-of-the-snow, but among those you might miss are the lovely *Anemone blanda* 'Atrocoerulea', the deep blue mountain anemone of Greece which does so well with us, and *A. pulsatilla*, the pasque-flower, a rare native, not a bulb but included here lest it be forgotten. There is no more lovely anemone. It is variable in colour, mainly subdued purples and lilacs. In April it will push up its flower heads clad in an elegant coat of silky hair; these open as an exquisite chalice of six sepals with a golden powder puff of stamems lying in its heart, at the end of the season when flowers in this part of the garden are all too rarely seen.

The meadow-saffron, like a giant rosy crocus, makes its appearance in September; *Colchicum speciosus* 'Atrorubens' is the best of the purples and *C. speciosus* 'Album' a fine white, indeed one of the best white flowers to be found in the garden.

Schizostylis coccinea, the Kaffir lily, is reminiscent of a montbretia or tiny gladiolus. It needs planting in a warm spot, where it will produce its spikes of 10 to 15 flowers from September to November. Usually bright red, it has a good pink form in 'Mrs Hegarty'.

The other area of the garden where bulbs are especially helpful is the mixed border – preferably a sunny one. The mixed border is a relatively new concept which probably has its origin in those cottage gardens which always seemed to be full of flowers. It has as its basis the best of the herbaceous plants, achilleas and aconites, anchusas and asters, astilbe and anemones, chrysanthemum and coreopsis, iris, hellebores and red-hot-pokers, nepeta, paeony, monarda, salvia, sedum, and sidalcea. All these together, with sub shrubs like fuchsia and veronica and some of the good grey-foliaged shrubs like santolina or senecio.

In this framework are left open spaces into which summer flowers like dahlias, antirrhinums, marigolds, etc, can be placed to provide cheerful colour to the task of the owner. Bulbs can have an important role in the changing beauty of such a border. One would expect to see groups of daffodils of varying form and flower time towards the rear; their dying foliage will then be screened as the other plants acquire their summer plumage. Tulips can be planted in the open spaces in autumn to be lifted and make room for summer annuals at the end of May. Later in the year one should see groups of gladioli; lilies such as *L. tigrinum*, *L. candidum* (the Madonna lily), and *L. regale; Fritillaria imperialis*, the crown-imperial; the summer-snowflake, *Leucojum aestivum; Galtonia candicans*, the Berg lily, which throws up 4 ft spikes with white pendulous bells, and many others.

As our interest is mainly with the warmer seaside gardens I want to draw your attention to a few which have suspect hardiness inland but beside the sea become a really good risk. The Guernsey-lily, *Nerine sarniensis*, is a good example. Any who doubt its ability to cope with seaside conditions may care to contemplate the story of its introduction to this country. Sometime in the middle of the seventeenth century a Dutch East India Company vessel which had presumably called at Cape Town was wrecked on the island of Guernsey. Several cases were washed ashore, where they broke open and the bulbs they contained were buried in the sandy shore by the tides. Their presence was undetected by the inhabitants until the scarlet flowers, in clusters of glittering, frilly trumpets, appeared to startle some passer-by. In the genial climate of Guernsey, even upon the shore, they flourished and eventually were marketed at Covent Garden.

Outside the Channel Isles one could not trust the hardiness of *N. sarniensis*, but *N. bowdenii*, which is a most attractive pink, is hardy at the seaside and well worth planting where it can grow undisturbed.

About a hundred years later another shipwreck, this time in Yorkshire, brought us the lovely Scarborough-lily, *Vallota speciosa*. Perhaps not so elegant as the Guernsey-lily, but its chalice-like form and glowing scarlet-red colouring, offset by a large white eye, are worthy of the really warm sheltered spot it needs.

A great many more *Agapanthus* will be grown when it is realized that the deciduous forms, especially those developed at Headbourne by the Hon. Lewis Palmer and known as the Headbourne Hardy Hybrids, become more widely known. They are certainly not worried by the smell of the sea, as those who have seen them luxuriating in great drifts on the grassy dunes in the Scilly Isles will realize. These hybrids vary in height from $1\frac{1}{2}$ to $2\frac{1}{2}$ ft with long, narrow, strap-shaped leaves, from among which are thrown the towering umbels of blue, open-trumpet flowers. The colour varies from pale blue to a deep, deep blue. The flowers appear about mid-August.

Another South African is *Amaryllis belladonna*. It needs a warm border because it is silly enough to throw up its leaves from January onwards. By June they have performed their function and die down to the very large bulbs. The flowers appear from nowhere, naked as the colchicums, in September growing to 18 in. or so in height. Eight to ten carmine, starry trumpets are borne on each purple stem. If you have to move them do so in June as soon as the foliage has died down.

I would certainly try to find a place for the angel's-fishing-rod, *Dierama pulcherrimum*, one of the most graceful of plants. Set out young plants from pots where it can grow quite undisturbed and away from tall plants that may obscure the delicate grace of the slender, graceful, arching 5-ft stems, strung with pendulous bells of purple, pink, mauve, or white. No wind perturbs it as the wiry stems seem proof to the worst the storm can do.

Sternbergia lutea is one of the finest of our autumn flowering bulbs. It bears brilliant, golden-yellow, crocus-like flowers in September. Plant it near the edge of the border where it will receive all the baking heat of the sun which is available.

Annuals

ANNUALS are plants which develop from seed and then flower, fruit, and die within a year. HARDY ANNUALS are those which can do this without artificial aid in the shape of greenhouse or frame, etc. They should be sown very thinly in March or April where they are to flower in well dug, not over rich soil. Cover lightly by raking in and protect from birds. Thin to the distance recommended on the packet as soon as the seedlings can be handled.

HALF-HARDY ANNUALS are those too tender to grow as just described but will thrive if given the shelter of a warm frame or greenhouse in their early stages, planting them out in late May or early June when danger of frost is over.

The growing of annuals in their hardy form is probably the cheapest form of colourful gardening. A well-dug border, a few shillingsworth of seed, a little patient picking off of dead flowers when needed and you can have a display full of interest from early July to October. In making your selection of species if near the sea, the wind is as always the limiting criteria; it is wise to avoid tall, soft species such as annual lupins or poppies and concentrate on the species which are naturally low growing – candytuft, etc – and on those with specially tough petals like the everlasting flowers – rhodanthe, etc.

Any which grow more than 12 in. high should be staked by the use of twiggy brushwood. These growths which can be clipped from the ends of pea boughs or often made from prunings in the winter if you remember, should be pushed into the ground 9 in. apart when the growing seedlings have their thinning out to about 4 in. apart. If your plant is to grow to 15 in. then your twigs' maximum height should be 4 to 6 in. less. The seedlings will grow up through the stakes, making a solid windproof mass. It may look as if you are cultivating twigs for a week or two but the result is worth it. A selection of dwarf annuals and 'everlastings' follows:

Abronia
Acroclinium
Alyssum
Anagallis
Arctotis
Asperula
Calandrinia
Chrysanthemum (annual)
Coreopsis (dwarf forms)
Dimorphotheca
Eschscholtzia caespitosa
Helichrysum
Heliophila
Helipterum
Iberis (Candytuft)
Limnanthes
Linaria
Linum
Mathiola bicornnis (Night Scented Stock)
Phacelia
Portulaca
Reseda (Mignonette)
Salvia horminum
Silene pendula
Saponaria calabrica
Sedum caeruleum
Ursinia
Xeranthemum

If you have greenhouse facilities this list can be extended by a wide range of half-hardy subjects. Really close to the sea the most salt susceptible species are the begonias, both tuberous and fibrous rooted, the French and African marigolds, nasturtiums, China Asters and anything else which raises its head above about 18 in. high.

Among the best half-hardy flowers are:

Ageratum	*Nemesia strumosa*
Antirrhinum (semi-dwarf)	Pansies
Gazania	Petunia
Heliotrope	*Phlox drummondii*
Lobelia	*Salvia splendens*
Matricaria	Statice
Matthiola (Ten Week Stock)	*Verbena venosa*
Mesembryanthemum	Zinnia (dwarf)

The Lawn

It is not the object of this note to explain in detail the making and maintenance of the well-kept lawn which is an essential feature of every garden. Be it flat or undulating, it is the green backcloth against which the other garden features display themselves. In discussing the main causes of failure I hope to highlight the different techniques advisable in coastal gardens.

1. Site preparation for seed or turf must be good. This is the only chance you have, as with tree planting, to break up heavy soils and to add moisture-holding humus to sandy or chalky ones etc. Grass roots may seem slender but they will travel many feet in search of food and water; give them a chance.

2. A lawn does not have to be flat. In many informal gardens it is indeed better to have rolling undulations, but do make sure they roll smoothly so that the mower can operate without leaving ridges or scalping high spots.

3. Sowing the right species of grass is especially important where sea breezes may deposit salt on the grass leaves. Grasses can be roughly classified into those which have flat leaf blades like the rye grass commonly used on playing fields and in pastures and those which have rolled

or folded leaf blades. These, the fescues, for example, are the species which have the ability to carry on the processes of living within their roll or fold whilst the outside copes with the weather.

A good seaside mixture is:

8 parts Chewing's fescue (*Festuca rubra commutata*)
2 parts browntop-bent (*Agrostis tenuis*).

Other grasses with these characteristics are – creeping red fescue (*F. rubra*), sheep's fescue (*F. tenuifolia*), hard fescue (*F. longifolia*). All have their uses but the recommended mixture is quite the best for uniformity of texture and colour.

An ample seed rate for this sort of seed mixture is $\frac{3}{4}$ oz per square yard. There are 5,000,000 seeds in a pound of browntop.

Do use a good seed. You may get a lot of impurities in cheap seed.

4. Turfing is the alternative to sowing grass seed. If your garden is really near the sea the temptation to quick results should be resisted, unless you can afford sea-washed turf, which contains the type of grasses resistant to saline conditions. Ordinary turf usually comes from meadows on a farm and is composed of grasses with big, broad blades as beloved by grazing animals. If you do turf, a really heavy top-dressing of sand and peat or a light, sandy soil well rubbed into the cracks and all over to a depth of $\frac{1}{8}$ in. is invaluable in preventing drying out and consequential shrinkage, with wide cracks between the turves. If cracks do appear, fill in rapidly with the same mixture and water well. Sea-washed turf is supplied in one foot squares. Start each alternate row with half a turf, *ie* 6 in. across. This will ensure that the cracks do not come opposite. Like the bonding of bricks this increases strength to resist movement by feet before the turves have knit together and helps to resist drying out.

Once you have a good lawn, the following will help to keep it so:

(*a*) Roll only in the spring to consolidate after the frosts and worms have puffed up the surface. Once is often enough.

(*b*) Buy a good roller mower (it is much easier to push) and set it to leave the grass $\frac{3}{16}$ in. (three pennies stacked) high, except for the first three cuts in spring at $\frac{5}{16}$ in. (five pennies). You can readily see this by turning the mower on its side and placing a straight board from the front roller to the back roller. The gap between it and the sole-plate, against which the cylinder cuts, is the height of grass left uncut.

(*c*) Mow regularly not more than ten days apart.

(*d*) Manure as lavishly as the pocket will allow. Three times at 2 oz per square yard of a good lawn fertilizer in early April, early June and late July.

Fruit

Fruit hates high winds; so do bees, which are such useful pollinators. Therefore it is advisable to omit fruit from your garden if you are near near the sea and in any case unless you can give protection from salt-laden winds.

If you do decide to try them, a strong application of commonsense to the problem will help you. Do not use standard trees for top fruits like apples and pears. Rather grow cordons, which in any case concentrate much fruit in a small easily-picked area. Alternatively, bushes on a root stock which will ensure they do not grow big – Quince C. for pears, Malling IX or 109 for apples, Mussel for plums, etc – is advisable. The soft fruits – raspberries, strawberries, gooseberries, currants, etc – are naturally relatively dwarf and can all find a place.

Vegetables

As with the fruit garden, commonsense in the choice of subjects plays an important part. Nothing enjoys being ripped about by high winds, so if there are alternative methods of cultivation, one of which allows for height reduction, this is advisable.

For example, in the case of runner beans the framework on which they are normally grown is a challenge to any wind; but they can be dwarfed so that no stakes are required. You can induce fruiting at about 2 ft by taking the tip out of young plants when about a foot high and then pinching the shoots a second time a month later; thereafter pinch weekly. A strip of polythene or straw on the ground will stop the soil being splattered on the beans by heavy rain.

Another tall crop is the pea. Here it is simple to cheat the wind by selecting heavy-cropping, dwarf varieties. You may need to sow more frequently to keep the succession going. Dwarf varieties of broad bean are also available.

I have already mentioned, right at the beginning of this book, the value of Jerusalem artichokes as a wind-filtering plant. Plant in February and allow 2 ft 6 in. between rows and 15 in. between the tubers which like to be 4 to 6 in. deep.

Within its shelter, wind and salt-sensitive subjects such as the tomato may be grown with the best chance of success.

One often sees it written that the seashore plants which have become popular vegetables are the most likely to succeed in the coastal garden. Indeed many of their names breathe of the sea – sea-kale; *Beta maritima*; seakale-beet; not forgetting asparagus. I am afraid that only gardeners with salinity trouble in the water table – *ie* the natural water level – are likely to reap any benefit. The vegetables mentioned will tolerate slightly salty water better than most, but for the most part they have forgotten their maritime past and demand the deeply cultivated, humus-rich soil beloved by most vegetables.

Dwarf Plants

It is difficult to over-estimate the importance of the ground-hugging plants. You will have seen from earlier chapters that there is an area of low pressure a few inches high above the earth's surface in which the fury of the wind is largely unfelt; even on top of a wall and hugging rock crevices in the rock garden these areas of calm amid the tempest offer a chance to grow plants which are naturally dwarf and have learned to keep their heads down from bitter experience. Of course, the ground must be well drained and cultivated so that root run is easy; given these simple requirements how may we carpet these seemingly inhospitable areas?

Few plants do better than *Aubrieta deltoidea*. Its very good nature almost anywhere makes it somewhat hackneyed, but if full use is made of the wide range of colour available an unforgettable springtime sight can be created. Cut it hard back soon after flowering and you will allow other plants to become the summer show and will never be faced with straggling slug- and snail-harbouring plants. Good cultivars include 'Belisha Beacon' (rose-red), 'Bressingham Red', 'Dr Mules' (violet-blue), 'Gurgedyke' (deep purple), 'Riverslea Pink', 'Triumphant' (mid-blue), and 'Wanda' (double red).

There are doubtless many of the enormous campanula family which are suitable, but *C. portenschlagiana* (which used to have the much more attractive name *C. muralis*, the wall campanula), is outstandingly good. Its rich blue flowers appear in late summer from tufty, deep-green foliage; it is one of the parents of 'Birch Hybrid', which has deeper flowers, held more erectly. Neither exceeds 8 in. Our wild bell-flower has a dwarf form, *C. glomerata acaulis*, which spreads by underground stems and will give a good account of itself.

There are few dianthus which cannot find a home here. *D. caesius*, *D. deltoides* 'Huntsman' (rich red and early), 'Little Jock' (rose-pink), and 'White Bouquet' are all good choices. Even a few of the border pinks can be tried, such as 'Doris' (pink), 'Ernest Ballard' (double red), or 'Ipswich Crimson'.

On a sunny or at any rate warm day there are few more spectacular plants than the *Gazania*. The commonest is *G. splendens*, which bears a profusion of orange daisy flowers some 2 in. across with an eye ringed in contrasting black. It has given rise to a large number of fascinating hybrids with flowers of white, lemon-yellow, orange, red, and brown, usually with a striking colour contrasting eye. They are not frost-hardy and must be over-wintered by cuttings struck in late summer. They can also be raised from seed, but the colours are pure chance and inevitably a number are unworthy. Like those of the mesembryanthemums, the blossoms are sensitive to temperature rather than the sun and are rarely open when it is less than 55°F (12°C). Take care you remove seed heads to promote continuous flowering.

The mesembryanthemums which are succulent, half-hardy plants, similar in requirements to the gazanias, have suffered at the hands of the botanists so that *M. roseum*, a somewhat harsh pink but gay and lively in the sun, should be *Lampranthus roseus*; other good species are *L. brownii* which is bright orange, *L. aurantiacus*, orange-red, and, of course, that little annual gem, *M. criniflorum* in a host of pastel shades of pink, orange, yellow, and blue. This has to be raised like any other half-hardy annual from seed and planted out when danger from frost has gone. Its common name is the Livingstone-daisy.

Other dwarf plants well worth your investigation include:

Armeria maritima (Sea Pink) – 6 in.
Convolvulus cneorum – 12 in.
Globularia cordifolia – 2 in.
Haplopappus coronopifolius – 9 in.
Helianthemum lunulatum – 6 in.
Helianthemum serphyllifolium – 4 in.
Helichrysum bellidioides – 3 in.
Helichrysum fontanesii – 12 in.
Helichrysum orientale – 8 in.
Helichrysum plicatum – 12 in.
Hieraceum villosum – 2 in.
Hippocrepis comosus 'E. R. James' – 6 in.
Iberis 'Little Gem' (perennial candytuft) – 6 in.
Iberis 'Snowflake' (perennial candytuft) – 9 in.
Limonium bellidifolium (statice) – 9 in.
Limonium cosyreuse – 6 in.
Micromeria corsica – 4 in.
Oxalis floribunda – 9 in.
Polygonum affine – 6 in.
Salix repens – 12 in.
Salvia argentea alpina – 12 in.
Sedum cauticola – 3 in.
Sedum spurium 'Shorbusser Blut' – 2 in.
Sempervivum (house-leeks). Try a collection. The names are most confused – 3 in.
Silene maritima fl.pl. – 6 in.
Silene schafta (catchfly) – 6 in.
Stachys lanata (lamb's-ear) – 8 in.
Verbena venosa – 12 in.

Index